MARCO ⊕ POLO

MUNICH

The best Insider Tips → p. 4

INSIDER TIP

Best of ... → p. 6

Sightseeing → p. 26

Food & Drink → p. 60

4   **THE BEST INSIDER TIPS**

6   **BEST OF ...**
- GREAT PLACES FOR FREE p. 6
- ONLY IN MUNICH p. 7
- AND IF IT RAINS? p. 8
- RELAX AND CHILL OUT p. 9

10   **INTRODUCTION**

16   **WHAT'S HOT**

18   **IN A NUTSHELL**

24   **THE PERFECT DAY**

26   **SIGHTSEEING**
THE OLD TOWN, LEHEL, MAXVORSTADT
& SCHWABING, GLOCKENBACH/AU/
HAIDHAUSEN, NYMPHENBURG &
NEUHAUSEN, OTHER DISTRICTS

60   **FOOD & DRINK**
FROM HEARTY FARE AND FUSION
COOKING TO HAUTE CUISINE

72   **SHOPPING**
WHERE BARGAIN HUNTERS AND
LOVERS OF LUXURY FIND WHAT
THEIR HEART DESIRES

SYMBOLS

INSIDER TIP	Insider Tip
★	Highlight
●●●●	Best of ...
☼	Scenic view
😊	Responsible travel: fair trade principles and the environment respected
(*)	Telephone numbers that are not toll-free

PRICE CATEGORIES HOTELS

Expensive	over 130 euros
Moderate	90–130 euros
Budget	under 90 euros

The prices are for two in
a double room per night
including breakfast

PRICE CATEGORIES RESTAURANTS

Expensive	over 18 euros
Moderate	12–18 euros
Budget	under 12 euros

The prices are for a main
course without drinks

On the cover: The Museum Brandhorst p. 48 | Fashion designed in Munich p. 80

CONTENTS

ENTERTAINMENT **82**
CULTURE AND NIGHTLIFE IN
ALL ITS MANY FACETS

WHERE TO STAY **92**
FROM EXQUISITE HOTELS TO
YOUTH HOSTELS: ACCOMMODATION
TO SUIT EVERY BUDGET

WALKING TOURS 102

TRAVEL WITH KIDS 108

FESTIVALS & EVENTS 110

LINKS, BLOGS, APPS & MORE 112

TRAVEL TIPS 114

USEFUL PHRASES 118

STREET ATLAS 124

INDEX & CREDITS 142

DOS & DON'TS! 148

Shopping → p. 72

Entertainment → p. 82

Where to stay → p. 92

Street atlas → p. 124

DID YOU KNOW?

Books & Films → p. 23
Gourmet restaurants → p. 64
Local specialities → p. 68
Relax & Enjoy → p. 78
Luxury hotels → p. 96
Keep fit! → p. 100
Budgeting → p. 115
Currency converter → p. 116
Weather in Munich → p. 117

MAPS IN THE GUIDEBOOK

(126 A1) Page numbers
and coordinates refer to
the street atlas
(O) Site/address located off
the map. Coordinates are also
given for places that are not
marked on the street atlas.
Map of surrounding area on
p. 138–139.
A public transportation map
can be found inside the back
cover

INSIDE BACK COVER:
PULL-OUT MAP →

PULL-OUT MAP 𝑀

(𝑀 A–B 2–3) Refers to the
removable pull-out map

The best MARCO POLO Insider Tips

Our top 15 Insider Tips

INSIDER TIP Jam Session

To the south of the city, high above the Isar, is one of the most popular beer gardens – the Waldwirtschaft. Where the 'beer garden revolution' began in 1995 reverberates today to the sound of jazz → p. 63

INSIDER TIP Olympic spirit

Everyone knows the Olympic Park but few clamber up the 55m (180ft)-high Olympiaberg mound to take in the view or have a drink in the little mountain hut → p. 59

INSIDER TIP Bavarian sushi

Ferdinand Schuster, a through-and-through Bavarian with a love for Japan, serves local Unertl wheat beer to wash down sushi, udon soup and yakitori → p. 67

INSIDER TIP Tête-à-tête

Romantic atmosphere, subdued lighting and plush niches for two – the intimate Hotel Lux offers an unforgettable dinner (not only) for lovebirds → p. 94

INSIDER TIP Bric-a-brac

Chamber pots, lederhosen, collectors' items and vegetable peelers – the Auer Dult is a real treasure trove. Three times a year the Mariahilfplatz turns into a colourful marketplace which magically draws people by the thousand → p. 110

INSIDER TIP Teatime

Oriental flair in the English Garden: in the Japanese teahouse you can take part in a traditional tea ceremony → p. 45

INSIDER TIP For the love of all things organic

Where once meat was prepared is now a culinary oasis, the home of Daylesford Organic with the emphasis very much on 'organic' → p. 69

INSIDER TIP Naughty but nice

A delicious deep-fried dough speciality – *Schmalzgebäck* – is prepared before your eyes: sinning is pure bliss in Café Frischhut → p. 63

INSIDER TIP **Do as the Romans do**

The decadent Roman-style restaurant Nektar, where you eat reclining, has expanded into the vaulted cellar next door. The chefs at the barbecue in Nektar Grill prepare everything from fillets of beef to tuna steaks → **p. 66**

INSIDER TIP **Asian party time**

The revamped, up-market disco P1 in the Haus der Kunst serves Oriental delicacies late at night → **p. 86**

INSIDER TIP **Heaven on earth**

High-quality produce from monasteries can be found in the delicatessen Genesis – from vinegars and oils to herbal teas and divine biscuits → **p. 76**

INSIDER TIP **Courtyard cinema**

When the sun in summer has set, the inner courtyard in the Gasteig comes to life: the Munich Film Festival is an invitation to watch films in an open-air cinema free of charge → **p. 52**

INSIDER TIP **Cocktails and jazz**

Not only heavenly cocktails are served in Mauro's Negroni Club with its classic bar décor, but also tasty Italian fare. Once a month (usually the 2nd Tue), talented jazz bands soon get people's feet tapping → **p. 84**

INSIDER TIP **Munich design**

The courtyard shop Vier Werkstätten sells mostly products by young, hip craftspeople and designers from in and around Munich. A place to browse and discover Munich's creative ans aesthetic spirit (photo left) → **p. 77**

INSIDER TIP **An oasis in the city centre**

The Hofgarten (Court Garden) is not just popular because of its lawns where people can sunbathe and children run about, but also for its wide gravel walks where you can play boules until well into the evening (photo below) or dance the night away in the Diana Temple → **p. 40**

BEST OF ...

FOR FREE

● *A feast for the ears and eyes*

The summer festival in July and August includes free concerts in the middle of the Olympic Park. The view of the lake and mountains is an added bonus → p. 111

● *Keep on rollin'*

Together with thousands of other inline-skaters you can take to the city's streets on Mondays. Roller blades and protectors are available free (on payment of a deposit) (photo) → p. 100

● *Theatre in the park*

The 'Münchner Sommertheater' performs classic plays in an amphitheatre in the northern section of the English Garden – free of charge and in a sociable, picnic-like atmosphere → p. 46

● *Tango in the open*

When the weather is nice in summer, tango dancers congregate every Friday evening in the Hofgarten. Anyone can and is welcome to join in! → p. 41

● *Concert evenings*

Cost-conscious music lovers meet at concert evenings in the summer at the Olympiagelände to listen to live music → p. 58

● *Yoga in the park*

Body and soul can be brought into harmony at professionally run, free yoga courses every Sunday morning May–Sept when the weather is good in Westpark. Finish off the session with a walk → p. 78

● *Training session*

It's virtually impossible for tourists to get tickets at short notice for a Bayern München match in the Allianz Arena, but you can easily watch Schweinsteiger and Co. training instead → p. 34

◉◉◉◉ Dots in guidebook refer to 'Best of ...' tips

ONLY IN MUNICH
Unique experiences

● *View of the Oktoberfest*
New York has its Statue of Liberty, Munich its Bavaria – personifying her homeland. She watches over the Theresienwiese and the raucous Oktoberfest. Climb up into her head and enjoy the view 18.52m (60ft) above ground level → p. 56

● *Bavarian breakfast*
A 'real' Bavarian breakfast is part and parcel of a visit to the state capital. Many locals go to the Großmarkthalle pub for their Weißwurst and pretzel, homemade sweet mustard and wheat beer → p. 70

● *La dolce vita*
The people of Munich live up to their reputation as the inhabitants of 'Italy's northern-most city' on warm summer evenings and gather on the city's squares, go for a stroll, or chat and relax in the open. This southern flair can be seen in particular on and around Gärtnerplatz → p. 52

● *Beer garden tradition*
When the weather permits, the locals like to spend their lunchbreaks in a shady beer garden too. The Chinesischer Turm (Chinese Tower) is especially well-known and popular (photo) → p. 62

● *Cult sites*
Both the Olympiastadion and the Allianz Arena are architectural masterpieces in which football history has been written which is brought alive on guided tours of the stadiums → p. 116

● *Traditional Bavarian costumes*
If you're after a genuine Bavarian costume or at least an accessory as a souvenir, it's worth seeking out the experts who can give you sound advice in a specialist shop, e.g. Ludwig Beck or Halfs → p. 76, 81

● *The sun god*
There's hardly any other city where the art of sunbathing is so cultivated as in the Bavarian capital. Regardless of the time of year, even the very first rays of sun bring people out to the street cafés, e.g. to eternally trendy Tambosi → p. 65

ONLY IN

BEST OF ...

AND IF IT RAINS?
Activities to brighten your day

● *Hollywood in Munich*
Buck up your spirits on a rainy day with a visit to Bavaria Filmstudios where you can immerse yourselves in the world of Falkor the Luckdragon in The NeverEnding Story, for example → p. 57

● *In the footsteps of history*
With a history stretching back more than 850 years, Munich has any number of weird and wonderful stories to tell, as well as artefacts to display. The exhibition 'Typisch München' in the Stadtmuseum, not only helps to understand how Munich's soul 'ticks', but it is also a particularly well devised multimedia trip through centuries past → p. 35, 104

● *Shop and dine*
Max Mara, Massimo Dutti, Dolce & Gabbana, Patrizia Pepe, Emporio Armani, together with top gastronomic delights and a cultural venue next door – this is what makes the Fünf Höfe shopping arcade so special. Architecturally interesting too (photo) → p. 79

● *Goings on in the Deutsches Museum*
You'll be able to spend any number of (rainy) days in the largest science and technology museum in the world as there is so much to try out between the mining section, physics department and the observatory → p. 51

● *Tram tour*
If the weather is not quite what it should be, take a ride across the city on a tram from which you can see any number of sites while keeping dry. The best route is the east-west stretch on tram no. 18 (from Gondrellplatz to Effnerplatz and back again), starting at the main station, a trip to Amalienburgstraße on tram no. 17, or to Effnerplatz on tram no. 16 → p. 114

RAIN

RELAX AND CHILL OUT
Take it easy and spoil yourself

● *Meditative*

Munich's oldest museum, the Glyptothek, doesn't just still our thirst for culture but is also a place to relax. You'll soon forget the hectic urban environment in the café located in a quiet and idyllic inner courtyard → **p. 46**

● *Historical spa*

Sweat it out in the sauna or the Roman-Irish steambath, relax in the silencium or swim a few lengths in fascinating Jugendstil surroundings. A visit to the Müllersches Volksbad, now more than 110 years old, is balsam for body and soul and an architectural delight to boot (photo) → **p. 52**

● *Guided open-top bus tours*

Double-deckers are now very much part of the Munich scene. Make yourself comfortable and listen to the guide from the bus' sun deck. For those who prefer things a little bit more individual: hire a rickshaw on Marienplatz → **p. 115**

● *Romantic evenings around a campfire*

Not far from Tierparkbrücke is the (in)famous Flaucher area where locals like to relax on beaches along the Isar. When the sun sets, hundreds of campfires paint a romantic evening picture → **p. 58**

● *Look no clothes*

If you fancy sunbathing in the nude, head for the English Garden, traditionally a nudists' paradise close to the city centre → **p. 45**

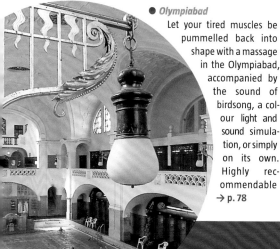

● *Olympiabad*

Let your tired muscles be pummelled back into shape with a massage in the Olympiabad, accompanied by the sound of birdsong, a colour light and sound simulation, or simply on its own. Highly recommendable → **p. 78**

INTRODUCTION

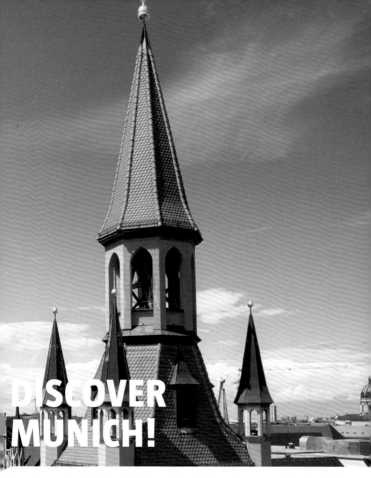

DISCOVER MUNICH!

On and around Marienplatz, in the heart of Munich, busy shoppers are elbowing their way through the department stores up and down the pedestrian precinct. On Viktualien-markt, on the other hand, just 200m away, the stands are closing. It's 6pm. A couple are seated at a wooden table in the beer garden in the shade of the chestnut trees. They both take a gulp of draught beer, squint into the evening sun, listen to the fountain splashing away and the natter of others at the tables around about, watch the market tenders clear things away, take a contented breath of air filled with the smell of barbecued sausage and unpack the radishes and pretzels they have brought with them. So this is it: la dolce vita – the relaxed calm to be found in Munich that is otherwise attributed to southern Europeans.

The Brenner Pass is indeed just a two-hour drive away and locals like it when their Munich is described as 'Italy's northern-most city'. The Italians on the other hand are

Photo: Marienplatz with the New Town Hall

welcome guests in the Bavarian capital and come in their thousands especially to the Oktoberfest and the Christmas market. Even if you share the Italians' love of Munich, you shouldn't 'do as the Romans do' at the same time: if you don't come to Munich at either of these peak times, you'll have a much better chance of getting to know the city and all its many facets.

That is, of course, if you don't head for the tourist honeypots but go off and explore the other districts, each of which can be very different from its neighbour and has its very own charm. Start in the old city centre around Marienplatz and Alter Peter, where the pulse of the Bavarian metropolis can be felt. From there it's just a hop, skip and jump to Munich's liveliest district around Gärtnerplatz that has evolved from a modest neighbourhood into a modern quarter for well-heeled artists, families and the gay community. In Maxvorstadt and Schwabing, by contrast, students, the culturally interested and bohemians mingle with the tourists. The greatest transition over the past few years has been in Westend around Schwanthaler Höhe above Theresienwiese. More and more artists and proprietors of small restaurants have moved into this former working-class district. The immigrant population of more than 35% here gives the district an international and creative flair. Such developments are typical of Munich,

> **Every district has a charm of its own**

A lovely place to meet up: drummers below the Monopteros in the English Garden

in fact, which has always been and still is lots of contrasting things at the same time – traditional and modern, conservative and socialist, FC Bayern and TSV 1860 München, families and single people, worldly and provincial, a hi-tech bastion and the home of traditional Bavarian culture with elegant districts and trouble hotspots, constant yet constantly changing.

The cliché of bearded regulars at the pub, celebrities and socialites is carefully propagated, but this image is gradually being merged with that of a young, foreward-looking city whose youth has rediscovered old traditions and reinterpreted these for

> **The younger generation has rediscovered traditional costume**

itself. One good example is the love of traditional costume. Many young people from Munich go to the Oktoberfest today in a dirndl or lederhosen – something that would have been unimaginable a few years ago. These include lots of people new to Munich working in the media branch, for whom the city has a strong attraction. Many try their luck in one of the 250 publishing houses here, for instance, of which Munich has the highest density in the world after New York. Ludwig-Maximilians-Universität and the Technische Universität have also contributed to Munich's reputation as a media and research centre. Both universities, with a total of around 88,000 students, are among the leading universities in Europe. The same is true of the Hochschule für Fernsehen

und Film (University of Television and Film) whose distinguished alumni include Oscar nominees and winners such as Caroline Link und Florian Henckel von Donnersmarck, strengthening Munich's position in the international film business.

Despite its cosmopolitan flair, the city is also known as the 'village of a million inhabitants' – and not without reason. If you turn off the main streets when out walking, you won't discover just a few roads that have a village-like atmosphere. And when the weather is good, you'll also notice how people are drawn outside – along the banks of the renaturalised Isar, into the many green municipal parks or just for a short rest on the nearest park bench. Go and join them and see for yourself what goes to make up Munich's attitude to life.

Number-wise, Munich is not quite as small as it may sometimes seem. The third largest city in Germany has a population of more than 1.364 million – still counting. Forecasters predict that the 1.5 million mark will be hit by 2030, naming the high quality of life and the many leisure opportunities as the main reasons that continue to attract high earners from business, politics and research. Many people who have settled in Munich give the city's location in the southeast of the country, its proximity to the mountains, lakes and open countryside as points in favour of moving here. With this expansion in mind, the city has already taken steps with one building project after another. Residential blocks above the Theresienwiese, former barracks turned into residential accommodation, the expansion of the Riem estate and on Ackermannbogen, to name but a few examples. On top of this, areas in and around the centre are being revamped – something that even tourists cannot fail but see. Right in the middle of the pedestrian precinct buildings are being demolished with new ones shooting up.

Subculture in a former department store

Munich has also had a make-over as a place to go out in the evening. While in the '90s nightlife shifted to party complexes on the edge of town, more and more clubs now are sprouting up in the centre. An empty department store, for example, could well find itself being used for some subcultural purpose or other – something quite unthinkable just ten years ago. Night owls ply up and down Sonnenstraße well into the early hours, passing bars, cafés, clubs and concert venues where the partying never stops. The range of cultural events on offer in the Bavarian capital is just as big. Opera, theatre, ballet and literature are as highly regarded as they have ever been and the festivals in particular, such as the Opera Festival, various open-air festivals and cinema screenings as well as the Tollwood Festival, are fixtures in the events calendar and attract thousands of visitors.

Culturally interested guests also get their money's worth in Munich, with its stone testimony to a history dating back more than 800 years. Here are a few key dates: Munich was first mentioned in documents in 1158 after Henry the Lion, Duke of Saxony and Bavaria, ordered the toll bridge in Freising to be demolished and had a new one built up-river in 'Munichen'. Market and minting rights were granted and Munich was founded. In 1255 the town became the seat of the Wittelsbachs whose influence can still be seen to this day. In 1632, Gustavus Adolfus of Sweden seized the city during the Thirty Years' War, whereas is was the Austrians who held sway for a brief period during the War of the Spanish Succession. 100 years later, in 1800, Munich was captured by Napoleon. Six years later, Bavaria became a kingdom and Munich its administrative centre. And King Ludwig II, the Fairy-Tale King, who is still revered by many a Bavarian to this day, did not only build castles in the air.

In the first half of the 20th century, Munich's role was not a glorious one. Although Kurt Eisner triggered the November Revolution here in 1918, a little while later Munich became the power base of the Nazi movement, with Hitler choosing the Hofbräuhaus as the place to found the 'National Socialist German Workers' Party'. Half of Munich was bombed flat during World War II, but bit by bit a new city emerged from the

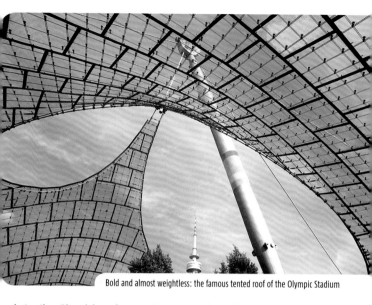

Bold and almost weightless: the famous tented roof of the Olympic Stadium

destruction. Olympiaberg, for example, was created out of a mountain of rubble. This large recreational area still exists today. This was where the Olympic Games were held in the summer of 1972 that hit the headlines after a terrorist attack.

The recent application for the Winter Olympics 2018 got the people of Munich talking again, as many were not in favour of the idea of staging the spectacle in Bavaria. For some, ecological awareness has priority over any possible economic

More and more people have adopted a 'green' attitude

considerations. More and more people in Munich have adopted a 'green' attitude with regard to fair trade, organic produce and environmental matters. Electric cars can be seen in the streets; only cars meeting certain emission standards are allowed within the inner ring road; and, anyway, locals prefer to cycle everywhere. People use their bikes whenever they can. The extensive network of cycle paths – more than 1200km (746mi) long – makes it possible for many to get to work by bike too. Of course, the predominantly good weather plays a decisive role too. Jumping on a bike to head off to a beer garden after work is simply part and parcel of life in Munich. And that holds true for any day when the weather's right. It would really be quite unusual if you didn't find yourself being swept along on la dolce vita wave too. The Spider Murphy Gang, one of the best-known local Munich bands in the 1980s, that is still popular today among the younger as well as the older generation, had a song 'Summer in the City' which went: 'I think my boss will have to manage without me today. Yes, I would much rather be lying with you in the grass ...'

WHAT'S HOT

1 Murder in Munich

Poirot & Co. Sleuth-style dinners where guests solve murder mysteries have been popular for some time. But how about a 'Headless Dinner' in *Zar Supper & Bar (Rosenheimer Str. 240, www.kopfloses-dinner.de)* instead? Or join other budding Miss Marples in *Klenze 17 (Klenzestr. 17, www.klenze17.de)* or *Niederlassung (Buttermelcherstr. 6, www.niederlassung.org, photo)* on Sunday evenings, when fans of the cult TV show 'Tatort' (Scene of the Crime) meet up to play at being detectives together. Great atmosphere even if you don't speak German.

More Meat 2

Fillets and tenderloins The steakhouse is making a comeback. While elsewhere the vegetarian trend is still en vogue, Munich is rediscovering the juicy steak. In *The Grill*, it's not just the food that is great but the atmosphere as well: super design and view too *(Lenbachplatz 8, www.the-grill-munich.de, photo)*. *Tabacco* is not only the best American Bar in town but also well known for its steaks *(Hartmannstr. 8)*. *Nero* is ideal for steak lovers with vegetarian friends in tow. Apart from wafer-thin pizzas, haunches of beef are also prepared in the wood-fired oven *(Rumfordstr. 34, www.nero-muenchen.de)*.

3 Electrifying

Setting the tone Munich leads the world when it comes to electronic music. The new top venue in town is *Bob Beaman (Gabelsbergerstr. 4, www.bobbeamanclub. com, photo)*. This is where the Munich record label duo *Permanent Vacation (www.perm-vac. com)*, among others, work as DJs. Even after moving premises, the 'small is best' venue *Harry Klein* still tops the list of electro clubs *(Sonnenstr. 8, www.harrykleinclub.de)*.

Balancing acts

Stand-up The surfers on the Eisbach in Munich are known throughout the world and have even been immortalised on the screen. But trendy sports fans have long since moved on – to stand up paddle boards (photo). Upright, paddle in hand, it's off down the Isar from Geretsried to Wolfratshausen, or – for the less adventurous – across one of the many ponds in the city. Boards can be hired from *Surftools* on Lake Starnberg *(Bahnhofsplatz 4, Starnberg, www.surftools.de)* or at *Surfers Spirit (Kolpingring 3, Oberhaching, www.surfersspirit.de)*. The *SUP Academy (www.sup-academy.de)* tells you where courses are held.

'In' district

Giesing In times gone by, Giesing was a modest, working-class district. But that's changing fast, as the creative-minded and high-earners have discovered this neighbourhood on the Isar not far from the city centre for themselves. Café-shop galleries such as *Café Lü (Hans-Mielich-Platz 2, www.treffpunkt-lue.de)* are opening for business and a trendy vegetarian restaurant is already there *(Charlie, Schyrenstr. 8, www.charl.ie, photo)*. In among them are the old, established and eternally cool meeting places such as *Prasserie*, that is intent on keeping its charm despite all the new-comers *(Sommerstr. 33)*. One man's meat is another man's poison: the group *Büf.f.e.l.* draws attention to the gentrification of the district with ironic poster campaigns *(http://bueffelmuenchen.wordpress.com)*. Demonstrations to save the historical football arena in Grünwalder Straße and the ensuing fight have paid off: the more than 100-year-old building will no longer be demolished.

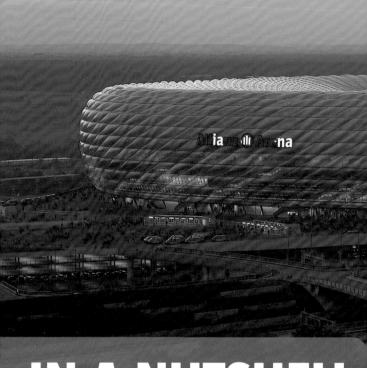

IN A NUTSHELL

BEER GARDEN

The typical Bavarian beer garden is shaded by chestnut trees (something that was important in the past to help keep the barrels in the cellar cool), gravelled self-service outdoor bar areas and the pleasant tradition of being able to bring your own food. This exceptional ruling in the gastronomic world – issued by Ludwig I – was originally intended to stop beer gardens being seen as competition for inns. The Bavarian beer garden regulations of 1995 state that: "Beer gardens fulfil important social and communicative functions, as they have always been popular meeting places for a broad spectrum of society, allowing people to come together in a relaxed environment regardless of social differences." The oldest beer garden in Munich, by the way, is the Augustinerkeller between the main station and Hacker-brücke that has been running as a pub and restaurant since 1854.

DIALECT

Who actually still speaks the Munich dialect – a kind of 'refined' Upper Bavarian? The former football player Franz Beckenbauer, nicknamed Der Kaiser (The Emperor), for example? Not really. His accent is more a mixture of the Munich dialect with a bit of standard German thrown

Beer gardens and *Weißwurst* – life in Munich is characterised by tradition but is also very laid back

in. Even if locals who speak dialect are no longer considered real rednecks and totally uneducated, linguists consider this variation of the central Bavarian dialect to be endangered. The facts: every year on average some 50,000 Germans and 30,000 foreign citizens set up home in the city as so-called Zuagroaste (new-comers). On the other hand, just a little under this number leave Munich for the big, wide world. How on earth is the Munich dialect supposed to survive? Some consolation can be found in the fact that Bavarian is widespread throughout the rest of the Free State and that the Munich variation is one of the best-loved dialects.

FÖHN

The 'Föhn' is a warm, dry downwind that, for many in Munich, is as good a reason as any if they need to put the blame on something for that horrible headache. The less weather sensitive look forward to such meteorological conditions when the skies are blue and, in winter, spring is in the air. Another fascinating effect is the view. When 'Föhn' is forecast, seek out higher ground as the atmosphere acts like a magnifying glass and makes it looks as if the Alps could be touched from the Bavarian capital.

FOOTBALL

The Munich football scene is like the classical colour theory for those who see everything black and white. You are either a 'Red' or a 'Blue' – or 'Grey' if you are really not interested in football at all. The borderline between the most successful German football club, Bayern München – the 'Reds' – and TSV 1860 München – the 'Blues' – is seemingly one that is impossible to blur. Paternal persuasion or personal preference for the never-ending success story or the underdogs can't be shed as simply as a sweaty football shirt. Despite the differences that are reflected in the league divisions they belong to and in the very different pay cheques they have, both teams play in the rubber-boat-like Allianz Arena in Fröttmaning. Bayern München display their magic to an eternally packed house at the top of the German football league table, whereas the 'Sechziger' play in the 2nd league and struggle to fill a third of the arena. But that does have one advantage: as a visitor, you'll be able to watch a match at short notice as there are always tickets available on the day for TSV 1860 matches.

ISAR

Admittedly, many other cities have been moulded more significantly than Munich by the river on which they have grown over the centuries. But even without mile-long riverside promenades, excursion steamers packed to the brim and festivals on the floodplains, the people of Munich are very fond of their special recreational area along the Isar – especially since the comprehensive renaturalisation scheme to the south of the centre has been completed, during which a natural river landscape with vastly improved flood protection measures was created. The wave on which surfers practice their tricks at the Flosslände in Thalkirchen has fortunately remained unaffected. According to legend, it was here in 1972 that two intrepid locals set out to find suitable places to surf in Munich. The Eisbach wave, that provides a perfect stage for board freaks in the English Garden, however, became much more famous later on. Time and again, wave riders test their skills in the fast-flowing torrent and try to hold out as long as possible against the raw power of the water. With varying degrees of success, of course – much to the amusement of the many spectators.

LAPTOPS AND LEDERHOSEN

A former President of Germany, Roman Herzog, coined the term 'laptops and lederhosen' when addressing Bavaria's shift from an agricultural state to a hi-tech region. Later, the conservative CSU party gratefully picked up on this sybiosis of tradition and the modern world in its election campaign. Party political interests aside, the term certainly captures Munich life quite succinctly. In the business sector, the city is in tune with the times and well positioned for the future. The people of Munich themselves don't let even the most exciting of innovations disrupt their everyday lives. They continue to value a more gentle and traditional lifestyle, without denying the advantages progress brings with it. The queue outside the Apple Store on Marienplatz, for example, at the launch of a new generation of products, can be just as long as that outside the Löwenbräukeller at its annual traditional 'Nacht der Tracht' event.

MÜNCHNER BIER

Yes, they still exist – the six true Munich breweries, namely Augustiner, Hacker-Pschorr, Hofbräu, Löwenbräu, Paulaner and Spaten. While Augustiner and Hofbräu München are still independent, the other breweries now enrich the product range of major international brewery concerns. Despite the increasingly global aspect and the less rigorous adherence internationally to Bavaria's purity law of 1487, Munich's breweries still keep strictly to the historical rule specifying the sole use of hops, malt and water, without any additives whatsoever. With such strong importance being attached to tradition, it comes as no surprise that 'Münchner Bier' has been a registered brand name since 1998. Nevertheless, it's worth peering over the top of your glass at regional breweries in the area too which also brew delicious beer, such as the Herzoglich Bayerisches Brauhaus Tegernsee (e.g. Tegernseer Hell), the Schlossbrauerei Kaltenberg (e.g. König Ludwig), the Brauerei Aying (e.g. Jahrhundertbier) and Brauerei Weihenstephan (e.g. Weihenstephaner Hefeweissbier), the oldest brewery in the world still in existence.

MÜNCHNER KINDL

The people of Munich are proud of where they come from and anyone born in the city can call him or herself a 'Münchner Kindl' – a 'child of Munich'. This is also the name given to the monk on the city's coat of arms that can be seen all over the place: on manhole covers, steins, trams, school buildings, beer bottles and right at the top of the Town Hall

The 'Münchner Kindl' is also on the city's coat of arms

tower. The 'Münchner Kindl' has also been a favourite motif for Bavarian artists since the 19th century, although the monk has gradually given way to a girl who, stein in hand and dressed in a yellow and black monk's habit, leads the procession of beer tent proprietors and breweries onto the Oktoberfest site. She stands next to the Lord Mayor when he taps the first keg and, when the Oktoberfest is over, acts as an official ambassador for Munich. Ellis Kaut, the inventor of the popular children's figure, Pumuckl, was once the 'Kindl' when young too.

Cheers! The Augustiner brewery float arriving at the Oktoberfest

OKTOBERFEST

It took place for the first time in 1810 on the occasion of the wedding of the later King Ludwig I to Princess Theresa of Saxony-Hildburghausen. Today, it is the largest collective hangover in the world breaking all records with regard to what is drunk and consumed. Beer is measured in millions of litres, chicken in hundreds of thousands. Vast crowds flock to the 'Wiesn' on Fridays and Saturdays when the beer tents are often closed due to overcrowding already late in the afternoon on Fridays and in the morning on Saturdays. By the way: the Oktoberfest largely takes place in September due to the better weather. Only the third and final weekend is actually in October.

OLYMPIC GAMES

The Summer Olympics in 1972, which were overshadowed by the frightful massacre of Israeli athletes by Palestinian terrorists, had an otherwise positive effect on the city. A positive picture of Germany was presented to the world 27 years after the end of the war. Munich gained architecturally spectacular buildings and an extensive public transport network. And what about the Winter Olympics? Having lost the competition for the games in 2018, consideration is being given to re-applying for 2022.

TRADITIONAL COSTUME

Some twenty years ago you could be certain that a man wearing lederhosen or a women in a dirndl was definitely from Bavaria, most probably from a rural area. In those days, traditional costume was frowned upon by the young people of Munich as a symbol of backward thinking. Today, you will come across lederhosen fans from the flat north of Germany as well as the traditionalists from the mountains with a Gamsbart (chamois beard) on their hats. What is very noticeable now is that local people are proud to display their traditional costume as a way of identifying with their roots. Even if they are not seen that often in day-to-day life, an estimated three-quarters of local residents who visit the Oktoberfest wear either *lederhosen*, calf-warmers and traditional brogues or a *dirndl* with a bodice and apron.

WEISSWURST

The locals' second breakfast is washed down with beer instead of coffee. Weißwurst – or white (veal) sausages – are ordered individually, not by the pair. The sausage is made largely of hacked veal, water and other secret ingredients and is gently heated in water and served with sweet mustard and a pretzel. The correct way to eat them is the source of heated discussion between warring fractions. The layperson cuts it in half down the length of the sausage. The hardy Bavarian picks up the sausage in his fingers, dips it in mustard and sucks out the contents. The expert, however, spears it, cuts it three-quarters of the way along and turns it elegantly inside out. It used to be said that the Weißwurst should be eaten before the clock strikes noon. Thanks to modern refrigeration, it can also be eaten later in the day now too.

BOOKS & FILMS

▶ **Gladius Dei** – Thomas Mann's wonderfully written novel set in Munich, vividly describing life in the city at the beginning of the 20th century.

▶ **We are Prisoners** – Oskar Maria Graf, German author and (later) US citizen, wrote several socialist-anarchist novels and narratives about life in Bavaria, most of which are autobiographical.

▶ **Keep Surfing** – Prize-winning documentary film by Björn Richie Lob that tells the story of the surfing scene on the Eisbach in the heart of Munich where river-surfing was invented 35 years ago.

▶ **One Day in September** – Simon Reeve's compelling and unblinking account of the Black September raid on the 1972 Munich Olympics that left five Palestinian terrorists, eleven Israeli athletes and one German policeman dead.

▶ **Rossini** – Set in a classy Italian restaurant in Munich, this densely plotted drama offers lush visuals, intrigue, sex, egos run amok and raw emotion.

▶ **Munich** – Steven Spielberg's Oscar-nominated film of the events during and after the terrorist attack at the 1972 Olympic Games.

▶ **The White Rose: Munich, 1942–1943** – Inge Scholl chronicles the heroism of her brother and sister, Hans and Sophie Scholl, and their friends in Germany during World War II. A testament to the power and courage of those who are willing to stand up for freedom and independence.

▶ **Chitty Chitty Bang Bang** – Baron Bomburst's castle in the famous 1968 feature film, based on Ian Fleming's book and starring Dick Van Dyke, is the 'must-see' world-famous Neuschwanstein Castle, south of Munich.

THE PERFECT DAY
Munich in 24 hours

08:30am A BAVARIAN BREAKFAST

A perfect day in Munich starts off early in the morning with a walk around the *Viktualienmarkt* → p. 79 when the stall-holders are setting up their stands and the first customers are out and about. Treat yourself to a glass of freshly-pressed fruit juice and one of the best pretzels in Munich at *Karnoll's Back und Kaffeestandl* or head off for breakfast at the *Weißes Bräuhaus* → p. 71 (photo left) in Tal.

10:00am CLIMB THE 'ALTER PETER'

Strengthened for the day ahead, running up stairs won't be too difficult. Just a few yards from the Viktualienmarkt, 306 steps lead to the top of *St Peter's* → p. 37, from where you have an excellent view of the centre of Munich.

11:00am GLOCKENSPIEL

Once back down again, go to *Marienplatz* → p. 34 and, together with many other visitors to the city, look upwards instead of down this time – at the glockenspiel on the New Town Hall that starts at 11am on the dot.

11:15am SHOPPING SPREE

How about some shopping now? Well-known high street labels can be found in Kaufingerstraße and Neuhauser Straße off Marienplatz, as well as the long established men's clothes shop *Hirmer* → p. 76 and the luxury department store *Oberpollinger* → p. 80. More brand names of the exclusive variety can be found on Theatinerstraße, e.g. in the *Fünf Höfe shopping arcade* → p. 79, that is also worth a visit for its architecture. While in the vicinity, take a look at the Late Baroque *Theatinerkirche* → p. 38 from the inside as well.

01:00pm LUNCH BREAK

The Fünf Höfen is not just a superb place to shop, but to eat too, e.g. in the Thai eatery *Kaimug*. Or else you wander a little bit further to *Tambosi* → p. 65 on the edge of the Court Garden. You can enjoy the Bavarian and international dishes served on the sheltered terrace as well as the sun in winter.

Get to know some of the most dazzling, exciting and relaxing facets of Munich – all in a single day

02:30pm AFTER LUNCH WALK

Odeonsplatz borders the *Hofgarten* → p. 40, where you can stretch your legs or stroll past the *Residenz* → p. 37. Don't forget to touch one of the lions outside (photo bottom left) which bring good luck!

03:30pm MODERN ART

Culture time: take bus no. 100 from Odeonsplatz to the museum complex in Maxvorstadt and sample the contemporary art in the *Museum Brandhorst* → p. 48 or the *Pinakothek der Moderne* → p. 49.

05:00pm TEA-TIME IN THE MUSEUM

Collect your thoughts over a cup of tea in the light-filled and architecturally impressive *Café Qivasou 48/8* → p. 49 in the Pinakothek der Moderne. Or try one of the many cafés on Türkenstraße or in the surrounding area just a few minutes walk away.

06:00pm THE PARK AND ITS DIFFERENT ASPECTS

Fancy a bit more fresh air? The perfect place for this is the *English Garden* → p. 44 (photo above right). Take bus 154 from Türkenstraße to Bruno-Walter-Ring and then on to the Chinese Tower. A few yards further and you'll find yourself in the midst of the after-work crowds moving between the beer gardens, the pond and Monopteros.

12:00pm ORGANIC DINNER

You can easily reach Fraunhoferstraße on the underground lines U1/2, from where you can choose between a number of restaurants within just a few minutes walk of each other. For fans of quality organic fare, try *Kranz* → p. 67, for example.

10:00pm BARS & CLUBS

Night owls will be attracted to the Glockenbach district with its renowned bars such as the *Café am Hochhaus* → p. 83 or else head for the clubs on *Sonnenstraße* → p. 86.

Start: Viktualienmarkt
Public transport: U/S Marienplatz
Tip: a MVV travel pass for one or more people can be recommended for the day

SIGHTSEEING

CITY **WHERE TO START?**
Marienplatz (127 D4)
(*⌕ H–J7)* and the Neue Rathaus are at the very heart of the city and just a 20-min. walk from the main station. Odeonsplatz and Maximilian-straße are just round the corner. All suburban line trains (S-Bahn) and the underground lines U3 and U6 stop at Marienplatz. Drivers can park in the multi-storey at Oberanger 35–37 not far from Sendlinger Tor. From there, Marienplatz is just a 5-min. walk along Sendlinger Straße.

If you want more than just a superficial impression of Munich, you will need a bit of time. The real beauty of Munich can only be found by letting its sights and day to day life in the city sink in and by seeing the city and its cultural highlights within the context of their history and inhabitants.

It certainly doesn't make much sense to try and 'do' the Residenz complex in. An evening spent in the Brunnenhof in the palace listening to a classical concert in the summer, an afternoon in Theatron in the Olympic Park with the rock musicians, the early hours of the morning spent with stallholders on Viktualienmarkt, a visit to

Photo: The Isar at Wittelsbacher bridge

Magnificent palaces, splendid churches, major museums and unequalled city parks: discover the many different sides to Munich!

Nymphenburg Park with a knowledgeable biologist, a wedding in the Theatiner church on a Saturday afternoon – this is where you'll find the city's real charm, well away from the typical tourist routes. Those interested in art will soon find themselves way off their carefully structured schedule – there is simply too much to look at! Excluding Berlin, Munich – with its almost 50 state-run, municipal and private art collections – has the greatest number of museums of any city in Germany.

THE OLD TOWN

The Old Town attracts tourists from all round the world who come to marvel at

MUNICH AT A GLANCE

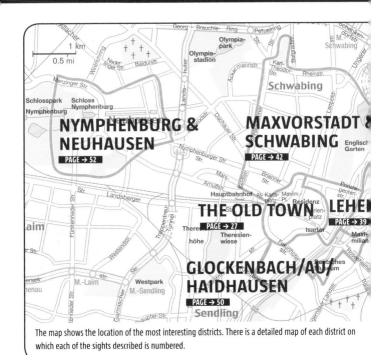

The map shows the location of the most interesting districts. There is a detailed map of each district on which each of the sights described is numbered.

Munich's famous landmarks, from its cathedral to the Hofbräuhaus. The main streets near many renowned sites in the historical city centre invite visitors to indulge in lengthy shopping sprees too. Marienplatz is at the very heart of Munich, around which the historical Old Town developed. The area around Dienerstraße, Weinstraße and Theatinerstraße was the former ecclesiastic centre and the home of nobility, as can still be seen today by the number of churches, old monastic buildings and town palaces. Walking towards Sendlinger Tor you will now find the flagship stores of well-known brands where merchants of old once went about selling their wares. The major shopping arteries, Kaufingerstraße and Neuhauser Straße, which lead to 'Stachus', are not necessarily blessed with architectural elegance, but you'll find all the large high-street chains in one place. To get to know the Bavarians joie de vivre and what makes them so special, you should definitely spend a little time at the Viktualienmarkt – the food market. This is where all the world and his wife meet – and where you can find the real Munich.

▮1 ALTES RATHAUS
(127 D4) (⌀ J7)

A look in the history books reveals that the first entry related to the Old Town Hall was made more than 700 years ago. Wars, fires and other catastrophes took their toll with the building being continuously altered. However, despite all its structural alterations, the glory of the

Town Hall – the late-Gothic barrel-vaulted ceiling by the master builder Jörg Ganghofer – has remained intact and still shows the artistic skill of the woodcarvers at that time. The INSIDER TIP *Spielzeugmuseum* (Toy Museum), which can be highly recommended, is housed in the tower of the Town Hall that was rebuilt in 1974. *Daily 10am–5.30pm | entrance fee 3.50 euros | U/S-Bahn Marienplatz*

■2 ASAMKIRCHE
(126 C5) (*ⅅ H7*)

A jewel of southern German Rococo architecture, built in 1733–46 by Cosmas Damian Asam and Egid Quirin Asam. It original name, St-Johann-Nepomuk-Kirche, goes back to the patron saint of bridges whose mortal remains are kept here as a reliquary. The Asam brothers were staunch Catholics and wanted to get that little bit closer to the Almighty by building this private church. They designed it in such as way that Egid Quirin could see the high altar through a window from his house

next door. The two ingenious master builders, however, had not reckoned with the people of Munich who protested fiercely against building a private church and ultimately achieved their aim of it being made accessible to everybody. *Sendlinger Str. 62 | U1/2/3/6 Sendlinger Tor*

■3 BÜRGERSAALKIRCHE
(126 B3) (*ⅅ H7*)

Although actually the Civic Hall, it has been used and called a church ever since a high altar was inaugurated in 1778. It is not only of historic interest due to its role as the former meeting place of the 'Marian Congregation', a religious group of priests and laymen close to the Jesuits. In the crypt of the church that was almost completely destroyed in World War II, is the burial place of Father Rupert Mayer, one of the principal figures behind the Munich resistance movement against Hitler. He was beatified by Pope John Paul II in 1987. *Neuhauser Straße 14 | U/S-Bahn Karlsplatz (Stachus)*

★ **Frauenkirche**
A city landmark with a mysterious footprint
→ p. 31

★ **Residenz**
The true heart of Bavaria → p. 37

★ **Englischer Garten**
A cool pint in an oasis of green → p. 44

★ **Museum Brandhorst**
A modern art museum that is a work of art itself → p. 48

★ **Pinakothek der Moderne**
The indisputable star among Munich's museums → p. 49

★ **Deutsches Museum**
For everyone who wants to know what, when and why something rattles, bangs or smells → p. 51

★ **Schloss Nymphenburg**
The magnificent Baroque palace of

the House of Wittelsbach → p. 54

★ **Allianz Arena**
A football temple for two rival teams → p. 56

★ **BMW-Welt/ BMW-Museum**
Futurististic building uniting the past and present → p. 57

★ **Olympiaturm**
When the wind blows from the south the view stretches to the Alps → p. 58

MARCO POLO HIGHLIGHTS

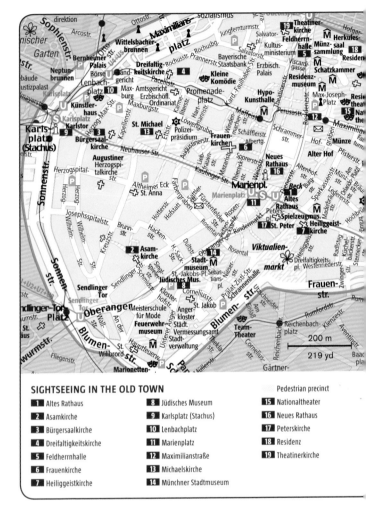

SIGHTSEEING IN THE OLD TOWN

1 Altes Rathaus
2 Asamkirche
3 Bürgersaalkirche
4 Dreifaltigkeitskirche
5 Feldherrnhalle
6 Frauenkirche
7 Heiliggeistkirche

8 Jüdisches Museum
9 Karlsplatz (Stachus)
10 Lenbachplatz
11 Marienplatz
12 Maximilianstraße
13 Michaelskirche
14 Münchner Stadtmuseum

Pedestrian precinct
15 Nationaltheater
16 Neues Rathaus
17 Peterskirche
18 Residenz
19 Theatinerkirche

4 DREIFALTIGKEITSKIRCHE
(126 C3) *(ɷ H7)*

Munich's first, late-Baroque Holy Trinity Church was founded in a typically Bavarian fashion. A valet's daughter, Anna Maria Lindtmayr, was so overwhelmed with visions of impending doom for the city brought on by the horrors of the War of

Spanish Succession, that she dedicated herself to the building of a church to assuage the wrath of God and spare her city. Citizens and representatives of the rural population were so impressed that they commissioned the Italian architect and court master builder, Giovanni Antonio Viscardi, to build the church. The unconventional interior, with its obliquely positioned columns and Cosmas Damian Asam's magnificent ceiling frescos, unites Italian vigour with Bavarian expressiveness. *Pacellistr. 6 | U/S-Bahn Karlsplatz (Stachus)*

⑤ FELDHERRNHALLE
(127 D2–3) *(ʍ J6)*

The colonnaded Field Marshals' Hall, erected in 1841 in the style of the Loggia dei Lanzi in Florence, was intended to honour the Bavarian army. On 9 November, 1923, Hitler's attempted putsch came to a bloody end here. After the National Socialists seized power in 1933, the Field Marshals' Hall became a cult site. A plaque to commemorate the so-called martyrs of 1923 was mounted on the east side and everybody passing it had to honour it with a Nazi salute. Those who didn't want to do this could get from Residenzstraße to Theatinerstraße via Viscardigasse, an alley running behind the Hall, and turn onto Odeonsplatz without having to salute. Even today this short cut is known as 'Drückebergergasserl' ('shirkers' alley'). The plaque was removed after the arrival of the Americans in 1945. Today, the Feldherrnhalle is not merely one of the city's many sights, but also provides a backdrop for a number of cultural highlights such as open-air classical music performances held in summer. *Residenzstraße 1 | U3/4/5/6 Odeonsplatz*

⑥ FRAUENKIRCHE ★ ☭
(127 D4) *(ʍ H7)*

It's proper name is the Cathedral Church of Our Lady and is the Episcopal church of the archdiocese of Munich Freising. The building of the cathedral was overseen by Jörg Ganghofer until its virtual completion in 1488, is 109m (358ft) long, 40m (130ft) wide and 37m (121ft) high and has (standing) room for 20,000 worshippers. Bearing in mind that the city had just

Is this really the work of the Devil? The mysterious footprint in the Frauenkirche

13,000 inhabitants at the end of the 15th century, it was clear to everyone at that time what importance the authorities attached to the cathedral. The gigantic structure was finally completed in 1525 with the addition of its bulbous domes on both towers. Over the centuries, the two onion towers of differing height have become an unmistakable landmark. Approaching the city from the south or west along the Munich–Garmisch motorway or Nymphenburger Straße, the towers can still be seen from the city boundary today, thanks to an old law prohibiting this view from being obstructed.

The most striking feature of the late-Gothic structure is its plain, almost austere appearance. Many myths enshroud the INSIDER TIP dark footprint at the entrance. Just before the cathedral was competed in the 15th century, the Devil sneaked into the building intent on destroying it. But then he saw that there were no windows – and thought that nobody would ever want to pray in a windowless church. Overcome by joy, he stamped his foot on the ground, leaving

Visitors, however, will find a wealth of ecclisiastical treasures such as the richly-decorated monumental tomb of Emperor Ludwig of Bavaria. An ascent of the tower *(3 euros)* is an essential part of any visit. *(April–Oct Mon–Sat 10am–5pm). Frauenplatz 1 | www.muenchner-dom.de | U/S-Bahn Marienplatz*

■ 7 HEILIGGEISTKIRCHE
(127 E4) (*Ⓜ J7*)

Together with the Church of Our Lady and St Peter's, the Church of the Holy Spirit is one of Munich's oldest places of worship,

Reflections in the window of the Jewish Museum

a clear footprint, and returned to Hell without touching the building. But he didn't go in far enough: from where the footprint is, it's true that no windows could have been seen at that time – but they were of course always there.

Opinions are divided as to whether restoration of the three naves carried out in the 1970s can be considered a success.

probably built in 1208 as a Romanesque chapel. It was rebuilt in the Gothic style after fire swept through the city in 1327 and, 400 years later, was given its Baroque pomp by the Asam brothers. Extensively damaged in the war, the church was painstakingly restored over a period of many years. *Prälat-Miller-Weg 3 | U/S-Bahn Marienplatz*

8 JÜDISCHES MUSEUM
(127 D5) (*ΩΩ H7*)

The monumental cube of the Jewish Museum not far from Viktualienmarkt has been open to the public since 2007. In the basement, the permanent exhibition 'Voices–Places–Times' gives an insight into Jewish culture in Munich and its history. The first and second floors are devoted to temporary exhibitions on various themes. The founding museum director, Bernhard Purin, is well known for highlighting Jewish history from unusual perspectives – a comic drawn by one artist, for example, traces Jewish life as it is today. *Tue–Sun 10am–6pm | entrance fee 6 euros | St.-Jakobs-Platz 16 | www.juedisches-museum-muenchen.de | U/S-Bahn Marienplatz*

9 KARLSPLATZ (STACHUS)
(126 B3) (*ΩΩ H7*)

Tram drivers still don't seem to agree on whether it's Karlsplatz or Stachus. Historically speaking, there is no doubt: the former Neuhausertor and the square beyond were simply rechristened Karlstor and Karlsplatz in 1792 to honour the Elector Karl Theodor. The inn-keeper, Mathias Eustachius Föderl, on the other hand, who ran the 'Stachusgarten' in 1728 on the site of what is now a department store, is probably to be thanked for the name 'Stachus'. There has always been a lot of traffic here. Where once the Salt Route entered the city, one of the busiest road junctions in the world evolved after World War II. Even today, Stachus is of central importance. While, above ground, caravans of cars and trams snake their way around the Old Town ring road, below ground, suburban line trains and the underground travel in all directions every few minutes. The building of these lines changed Karlsplatz below ground too. Until 2007, architecture typical of the 1970s dominated. Now, bright colours have taken over, modern boutiques and countless trendy food shops characterise this nodal point between the main station and Marienplatz.

To the east, on the right of the neo-Baroque shops designed by the architect Gabriel von Seidl, is the three-arched *Karlstor*, a remnant of the 14th century fortifications and gateway to Neuhauser Straße and the pedestrian precinct. The *Pini Haus* opposite, the rounded corner building, has become a city landmark. Below ground level, a busy shopping mall has been created. Where Stachus runs into the Lenbachplatz to the north, the gleaming white Justizpalast (Palace of Justice) can be seen. Built in the 19th century by the architect Friedrich von Thiersch (1852–1921), it is a tribute in stone to Gothic, Renaissance and Baroque architecture. *U/S-Bahn Karlsplatz (Stachus)*

10 LENBACHPLATZ (126 B3) (*ΩΩ H7*)

Built around the turn of the 20th century and typical of the lively urban planning of the day that did not let itself be subjected to any ideology. The opulently designed *Lenbachbrunnen* in the middle of the square, flanked on both sides by larger-than-life figures, is an inviting spot. Thanks to its atmospheric illumination, the fountain is a popular snapshot especially at night. The *Künstlerhaus* opposite, by Gabriel von Seidl, was the meeting place of the artists' society for many years. On the other side of the road, next to the former Bayerische Börse (Bavarian Stock Exchange) which now houses the Heart Club, is *Bernheimer Palais*, built in 1889–91 by Friedrich von Thiersch. This building, once owned by the Bernheimer family of merchants, was opulently renovated in the '90s and is now occupied by elegant shops, offices and hairdressers. *U/S-Bahn Karlsplatz (Stachus)*

11 MARIENPLATZ (127 D4) *(ff H–J7)*
Munich's social, economic and architectural heart since it's earliest days. The *Mariensäule* (St Mary's Column) was erected in 1638, the fulfilment of a vow taken by the devout Elector Maximilian I to establish a foundation, should Munich and Landshut survive the Swedish campaign during the Thirty Years' War unblemished. Today, Marienplatz is not only a must on every tourist's list of places to see, especially because of the glockenspiel in the New Town Hall at 11am and noon – and 5pm March–Oct – it is also the venue of almost every conceivable cultural event in the city. Officially approved street musicians, jugglers and mime artists here (and on adjacent Neuhauser Straße) put all their energy into their acts and earn a pretty penny too. The *Fischbrunnen* (Fish Fountain), to one side of the square, is not only a popular meeting place, but has also been the site of an annual ritual since 1426 – 'the washing of the purse'. According to legend, anyone washing his 'money bag' here on Ash Wednesday will not have any financial problems. And so it's quite obvious why the Lord Mayor of Munich is always at the front of the queue when wash-time comes round again. *U/S-Bahn Marienplatz*

12 MAXIMILIANSTRASSE
    (127 E–F3) *(ff J–K7)*
Munich's showcase street also reveals much about the conflicting nature of this city. Just 1.5km (1mi) long, it is still regarded as one of the great boulevards. It begins, looking eastwards, highly symbolically. At right angles to the pedestrianised Residenzstraße, it stretches towards the rising sun; to the left it is flanked by the Residenz and the Nationaltheater. Maximilian II, disgusted by his father's love of pure neo-Classicism, realised his vision of a more liberal architecture. In 1853, the court architect Friedrich Bürklein, dared to make an architectural cocktail of styles incorporating Tudor Gothic, Italian Renaissance elements and French arcades. After World War II, the people of Munich managed to wrest this royal concept from the rubble. Standing in the morning facing the sun, you will see the Classicist seat of the Bavarian State Parliament rising above the Isar, the Maximilianeum – an almost utopian vision. In between, Munich's most expensive fashion boutiques can be found, plus a few high-class jewellers, top hairdressers and classy

LOW BUDGET

▶ For 1 day or 3, you can travel either alone (9.90/19.90 euros), or with up to 4 others (16.90/29.90 euros) on all underground and suburban lines (U/S-Bahn), trams and buses using the *City Tour Card* in the whole of the inner-city zone, or in the entire local network (3 days 31.50 euros, groups 51.50 euros). This also entitles you to reductions at more than 45 museums and sights. *www.citytourcard.com*

▶ On Sundays, the entrance fee to a lot of museums is only 1 euro.

▶ Football fans can get close to their stars and watch them ● training. And all for nothing of course! Perhaps you can even get an autograph for free too *(FC Bayern Munich | (139 F2) (ff H/J 12) | Säbener Str. 51–56 | www.fcb.de; TSV 1860 Munich | (139 E2) (ff H 12) | Grünwalder Str. 114 | www.tsv1860. de; both: tram 15/25 Südtiroler Straße*

bistros, the elegant Kempinski Vier Jahreszeiten hotel and the city's highly-praised theatre, the Munich Kammerspiele. The Upper Bavarian parliament sits the other side of the monument to Maximilian II, who defiantly and proudly personifies the ideology of the day: justice, military strength, peace and science. *Tram 19, U/S-Bahn Marienplatz or U4/5 Lehel*

▮13▮ MICHAELSKIRCHE (126 C3) *(⌖ H7)*

Never at a loss when it came to self-promotion, Duke William V set about creating an imposing monument to the Counter Reformation in the form of this church and plundered the state coffers to do so.

▮14▮ MÜNCHNER STADTMUSEUM
(127 D5) *(⌖ H7)*

Munich City Museum is not a local-history museum in the true sense of the word. Like in a time machine, you are taken on a journey through the centuries and witness the city's development from a royal seat to a cosmopolitan metropolis, its domestic culture in the 19th and 20th centuries, the end of National Socialism and Munich's emergence as a centre for the media industry. The audio tours *(3.50 euros)*, tailored to the individual exhibitions, can be heartily recommended. ● In addition to the excellent permanent exhibition 'Typisch München', temporary

Munich's short but elegant boulevard: Maximilianstraße

He could later credit himself with the construction – for 'his Jesuits' – of the second-largest barrel-vaulted church in the world after St Peter's in Rome, a structural miracle by the standards of the day. The crypt contains the tombs of a number of Bavarian rulers, including Ludwig II. Munich's best church choir can be heard here on Sundays *(see local press for details). Maxburgstr. 1 | U/S-Bahn Karlsplatz (Stachus)*

exhibitions are regularly held on subjects to do with the city, the region and art. A detour to the *Servus-Heimat Souvenirshop* is well worthwhile as is a look at the trinkets sold at the INSIDER TIP original 'Auer-Dult' fair booth. Here you can find unusual and funny articles that make perfect gifts. *Tue–Sun 10am–6pm | entrance fee 4 euros | St. Jakobs-Platz 1 | www.stadtmuseum-online.de | U/S-Bahn Marienplatz*

The Nationaltheater is equally elegant inside too

15 NATIONALTHEATER
(127 E3) (*∅ J7*)

At the beginning the the 19th century, Bavaria's first king, Maximilian I Joseph, wanted to have a theatre in the style of the Odéon in Paris and commissioned the young architect Karl von Fischer to build it. Just five years after its official opening in 1818, a devastating fire destroyed the majestic, austere, Classicist building and Leo von Klenze set about reconstructing the temple to the arts. World War II, however, saw the destruction of the building for a second time. Instead of agreeing to a modern replacement, the city fathers decided in favour of reconstructing it yet again. As the magnificent semi-circular auditorium only seats 2100, each seat has to be subsidised to the tune of more than 100 euros for each performance in order to maintain the high standard of productions. The more recent history of the theatre, nevertheless, has been an honourable one indeed: Richard Strauss directed four world premieres here, conductors such as Clemens Krauss, Bruno Walter, Hans Knappertsbusch, Solti, Fricsay and Keilberth launched their global careers from within these walls. The musical director, Kent Nagano, will remain until 2013. The highlight of the season is the Opera Festival in July. *Advance booking for tours: tel. 089 2185 01 | Max-Joseph-Platz 2 | 6 euros | www.bayerische.staatsoper.de | tram 19 Nationaltheater*

16 NEUES RATHAUS ☀
(127 D4) (*∅ H–J7*)

An excessive enthusiasm for all things Gothic inspired the Graz-based architect, Georg von Hauberrisser, to his rather bizarre ideas when working on the New Town Hall between 1867 and 1908. It houses the fourth largest glockenspiel in Europe in its 80m (262ft)-high tower. Everyday at 11am and noon (March–Oct, also at 5pm), it tells the story of two major events which took place on Marienplatz: the tournament to celebrate the wedding of Duke William V of Bavaria to Renata of Lorraine (1568), and the Coopers' Dance which is still danced today every seventh year at carnival time. As the tale goes, is was the coopers who, with their traditional dancing, got the citizens of Munich to leave their houses once again at the time of the Plague and put the dormant social life in the city back on its feet again. *Lift in tower May–Oct daily 10am–7pm, Nov–April Mon–Fri 10am–5pm | 2.50 euros | U/S-Bahn Marienplatz*

17 PETERSKIRCHE ☀️
(127 D4) (*M J7*)

One of Munich's oldest buildings, known as 'Old Peter', and (in)famous for its 306 steps to the dizzying heights of the viewing platform. Long before the founding of the city, a chapel stood on 'Petersberg'. Over the centuries, an architecturally interesting combination of Romanesque, Gothic, early Baroque and Rococo styles emerged which attracts many to listen to the wonderful Mozart and Haydn masses celebrated mostly on Sundays and public holidays. But even during the week, St Peter's is an oasis of peace and quiet, providing a refuge from the bustle of the city centre and boasts a wealth of precious objects from the workshops of famous artists such as Erasmus Grasser who carved the marble tombstones. Nikolaus Gottfried Stuber created the high altar; the sedile to the right of the altar and the Mariahilf Altar in the South Nave were made by the Workshop of Ignaz Günther. *Tower open in summer Mon–Fri 9am–6.30pm, Sat, Sun 10am–6.30pm, winter Mon–Fri 9am–5.30pm, Sat, Sun 10am–5.30pm | 1.50 euros | Rindermarkt 1 | www.alterpeter.de | U/S-Bahn Marienplatz*

18 RESIDENZ ⭐ (127 E2–3) (*M J6–7*)

The Munich Residence impresses visitors due to its sheer overwhelming grandeur. We recommend planning at least one whole day for a visit to this, the largest palace building in the centre of a city in Germany. After being badly damaged in World War II, the Free State poured millions into restoring the 'cultural heart' of Bavaria, the seat of the ruling dynasty for five hundred years, back to its former glory. Every architectural style that constitutes Bavarian cultural history can be found here: austere Renaissance, extravagant Baroque, playful Rococo and linear Classicism.

In 1385 the foundation stone was laid for the 'Neuveste' (new fortress) in the northeast of the old city. Over the centuries the Residence, comprising three main complexes and six courtyards, evolved step by step. If you haven't enough time to look at all the treasures between Residenzstraße, the Hofgarten and Marstallstraße, you should at least visit the *Residenzmuseum*, one of Europe's most exquisite royal art collections. The vestibule, portrait gallery, china collection, 'Antiquarium' (which is used today by the Minister President for state receptions), the porcelain rooms, the 'Reiche Zimmer', Mirror Room and the Nibelungen Halls provide

The magnificent heart of Bavaria: the Residenz

a general overview. A INSIDER TIP combined ticket for the Residenzmuseum and the Schatzkammer *(11 euros)* can be recommended, that also includes entrance to the crown jewels and other exquisite pieces. *April–Oct daily 9am–6pm, Nov–March daily 10am–5pm | entrance fee Residenzmuseum 7 euros, Schatzkammer 7 euros | Residenzstr. 1a | www.residenz-muenchen.de | U/S-Bahn Marienplatz, tram 19 Nationaltheater*

19 THEATINERKIRCHE
(127 D2) (*M J6*)

The birth of Max Emanuel must have been an event of unparalleled importance for his parents, Elector Ferdinand Maria and Henriette Adelaide. Not only did the baby's father present the mother with Nymphenburg Palace, but the couple also commissioned one of Munich's finest churches and dedicated it to St Cajetan (the founder of the Theatine Order). Since the saint and the order both originated in Italy, the architecture echoes the elegant Italian High-Baroque. Some 100 years after laying the foundation stone, François Cuvilliés fitted it out in the Rococo style. The Theatine Church is one of the most striking features of the Munich skyline together with St Ludwig's and the Church of Our Lady. Particularly impressive are the high altar with its painting of the Madonna by Caspar de Crayer, a pupil of Rubens', the superbly executed black pulpit and the royal crypt of the Wittelsbachers' under the high altar. If you would like to find out more about the history of the church and can speak German, you can book a tour run by the Münchner Bildungswerk *(5 euros | www.muenchen.keb-muenchen.de)*, given by a knowledgable art historian. *Theatinerstr. 22 | U3/4/5/6 Odeonsplatz*

The Theatinerkirche's Rococo façade was only completed 100 years after its inauguration

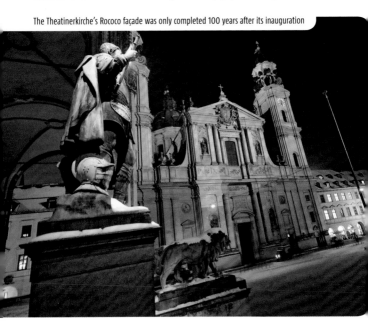

LEHEL

This district was once the home of day-labourers who were too poor to live within the city walls. Now, the old buildings have been renovated, the façades cleaned, and it has become a popular place to live close to the city centre.

Most visitors are drawn to Prinzregentenstraße where the Haus der Kunst, the Schack Galerie and the Bayerisches Nationalmuseum are virtually next to one other. Following this grand boulevard towards the city centre, visitors are rewarded with a fantastic view of the Bayerische Staatskanzlei (State Chancellery) that was formerly a military museum. It is situated on the edge of the English Garden which begins in Lehel.

■ BAYERISCHES NATIONALMUSEUM
   (135 D1) (*Ø K6*)

Those interested in the art and cultural history of Bavaria and southern Germany should not miss the National Museum. It is three museums rolled into one: an art-historical museum (western art, especially sculpture from the early Middle Ages up to the mid-19th century), an arts and crafts museum (with specialist collections of porcelain, ceramics, cut stones, gold and silverwork, painting on glass, clocks, miniatures, etc.), and a cultural museum (folk art, religious art, crib collection). Of particular note are the sculptures by Tilmann Leinberger, pictures by Grasser and Polack, the Ignaz Günther Room, the Landshut and Schwanthal Rooms, the Tattenbach Collection and the Augsburg weavers' workshop on the ground floor. There is also a comprehensive collection of Meissen and Nymphenburg porcelain as well as farmhouse parlours, masks and potters' tools. The crib collection features more than 6000 figures and is unrivalled any-

where in the world. *Tue–Sun 10am–5pm, Thu 10am–8pm | entrance fee 7 euros | Prinzregentenstr. 3 | www.bayerisches-nationalmuseum.de | U4/5 Lehel, tram 18 Nationalmuseum*

■ HAUS DER KUNST
   (134 C1) (*Ø J6*)

There used to be a predecessor to the neo-Classicist temple to the arts back in 1854 on Königsplatz. 35 years later, fire destroyed the huge crystal palace where the 'First German General and Historical Art Exhibition' was held in 1858. A decision was quickly made to erect a new building, but this took its time. In 1933, without further ado, Hitler chose a new site for the building on the southern edge of the English Garden, and the 'Haus der Deutschen Kunst' was opened in 1937. During the Nazi regime, only works of art that propagated the 'blood and soil' ideology were exhibited. This changed abruptly after the end of World War II, and from 1949 onwards, artists such as Vassily Kandinsky, Paul Klee and Pablo Picasso – who had previously been labelled 'degenerate' – set the tone. At the same time the Americans also used part of the building as an officers' club.

Many exhibitions and decades later, a big coup was made in the appointment of the Belgian Chris Dercon as director (2003–2010). Not only did he manage to return the central hall to how it was in 1937 – a highly controversial undertaking – but he also attracted names such as the world-acclaimed Chinese artist Ai Weiwei to Munich. It is also thanks to his efforts that the Haus der Kunst has regained its global importance through a very successful mixture of exhibitions on architecture, design, fashion, photography and film. This is now being continued by his successor, the Nigerian-born Okwui Enwezor. *Fri–Wed 10am–20, Thu 10am–10pm | entrance fee*

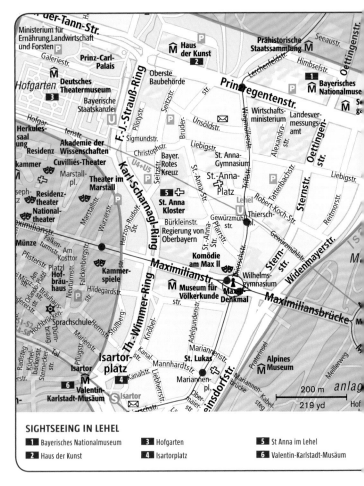

SIGHTSEEING IN LEHEL

1 Bayerisches Nationalmuseum
2 Haus der Kunst
3 Hofgarten
4 Isartorplatz
5 St Anna im Lehel
6 Valentin-Karlstadt-Musäum

*from 5 euros depending on exhibition |
Prinzregentenstr. 1 | www.hausderkunst.de |
tram 18, bus 100 Haus der Kunst*

3 INSIDER TIP HOFGARTEN
(127 E2) (ⓓ J6)

The Court Garden is a green oasis linking
Odeonsplatz with the English Garden and
was laid out by Elector Maximilian I around
1617. The Italianate Renaissance garden,
flanked by the Bavarian State Chancellery
and the Residenz, has evolved into a popular place to relax. Boules players show off
their skills on the broad gravel paths (and
if you fancy trying it yourself, boules sets
can be hired at the Tambosi beer garden
pavilion), children play on the lawns,
stressed-out managers bathe in the sun
and the more energetic dance ● tango
(Fri), salsa *(Wed, Sun)* or swing *(Sun after-*

noon), gliding over the marble floor in the Diana Temple in the centre of the garden. This is also where you can find the Kunstverein Munich *(www.kunstverein-muenchen. de)* and the historical *Kaffeehaus Luigi Tambosi* (founded in 1775), that offers opera and dinner under the arcades from May–Sept on Thu from 7pm *(www.tambosi.de)*. U3/4/5/6 Odeonsplatz

◪ ISARTORPLATZ
(127 F5) *(ΩΩ J7)*

Isartor (Isar Gate), erected by the Holy Roman Emperor, Louis IV (the Bavarian), along with the second city wall (1285–1347), marks the border between the historical Old Town, the Isarvorstadt district and Lehel. It is the only city gate that is still complete. Since 1959, the left-hand tower has housed the *Valentin-Karlstadt-Musäum.* Further remnants of the city wall can be seen in the administrative centre of the Stadtsparkasse bank next door.

To the left of Isartor, on the edge of the lawned area, the wonderfully cosy little inn INSIDER TIP *Isarthor (daily | Kanalstr. 2 | www.gasthaus-isarthor.de)* serves excellent roast pork. *S-Bahn Isartor*

◪ ST ANNA IM LEHEL
(134 C2) *(ΩΩ J7)*

Not only one of its most significant but also Bavaria's first Rococo church. Badly damaged in World War II, it was later beautifully restored in several phases. It was begun in 1727 by Johann Michael Fischer and took five years to complete. Fischer's new architectural feature: the oval-shaped interior. The Asam brothers contributed the decorative frescos to the vaulted ceiling and the altarpieces which have been painstakingly reconstructed based on the originals. *St.-Anna-Platz 5 | U4/5 Lehel*

Sunday is swing time: dancers demonstrate their skills in the Diana Temple in the Hofgarten

MAX-VORSTADT & SCHWABING

Maxvorstadt is Munich's university and museum district and is popularly known as 'Munich's brain'. This is where Ludwig I let his vision of 'Athens on the Isar' be turned into reality in the 19th century. Even today, the Classicist buildings dominate the architecture of this part of the city.

Commemorating the comedian: the Valentin-Karlstadt-Musäum

◼ 6 VALENTIN-KARLSTADT-MUSÄUM
(127 F5) (∅ J7)

The tower to the left of Isartor houses one of Munich's most entertaining museums dedicated to the comedian and actor Karl Valentin and Liesl Karlstadt. Apart from the nail on which Valentin hung up his profession and his winter toothpick wrapped in fur, this collection of curiosities has a number of prime specimens as well as documenting the popular theatre of its day in an imaginative way. Since early 2000, Petra Perle – a whacky local comedienne – rules the roost in the INSIDER TIP *Turmstüberl*, a folk-singers' café with furnishings from Café Größenwahn, a legendary fin-de-siècle coffeehouse. Free admission to pensioners over 99 accompanied by their parents! Guided tours every even Sat in the month at 3.01pm. *Mon, Tue, Thu 11.01am–5.29pm, Fri, Sat 11.01am–5.59pm, Sun 10.01am–5.59pm | entrance fee 2.99 euros | Tal 50 | www.valentin-musaeum. de | S-Bahn Isartor*

Together with its new additions – the Pinakothek der Moderne, the Museum Brandhorst and the Sammlung Ägyptischer Kunst – there are now 17 museums in all on Munich's new 'Kunst Areal' museum area that lies between Adalbertstraße and Königsplatz. It provides an excellent overview into the various historical aspects of art and cultural history. The serious and the light-hearted rub shoulders here: whoever wants to recover after a history and art tour will find any number of cafés, pubs and galleries near the museums and university which are well frequented by students and academics.

Directly to the north is Schwabing. Munich's legendary district, where artists had riotous parties back in the 'Roaring Twenties' and where 'in' clubs such as the Klappe were a guarantee for scandal in the '70s, has now lost much of its glamour. The Spider Murphy Gang's song 'Schickeria' has its roots in Klappe and immortalises the former celebrity meeting-place. 'See and be seen' however is still the motto that dominates Leopoldstraße. During the day, the fashion-conscious rummage through the countless boutiques on the lookout for trendy gear; at night, the mass of clubs, bars and restaurants makes the choice difficult.

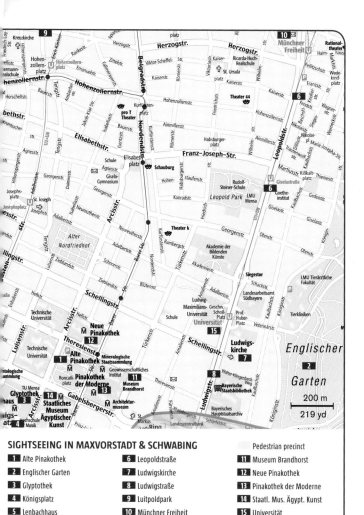

SIGHTSEEING IN MAXVORSTADT & SCHWABING

1 Alte Pinakothek
2 Englischer Garten
3 Glyptothek
4 Königsplatz
5 Lenbachhaus

6 Leopoldstraße
7 Ludwigskirche
8 Ludwigstraße
9 Luitpoldpark
10 Münchner Freiheit

░ Pedestrian precinct
11 Museum Brandhorst
12 Neue Pinakothek
13 Pinakothek der Moderne
14 Staatl. Mus. Ägypt. Kunst
15 Universität

1 ALTE PINAKOTHEK
(134 B1) *(ᗰ H6)*

Among the 1400 paintings by Old Masters in the Alte Pinakothek you won't find Leonardo da Vinci's Mona Lisa, but his Virgin and Child with a Vase of Flowers instead and Lorenzo Lotto's Mystic Marriage of St Catherine. The Alte Pinakothek is one of the most important art galleries in the world. All schools of European painting from the Middle Ages until the early 19th century are represented in its holdings. The focus of the collection is on 15th and 16th-century German and Netherlandish painting, 17th-century Dutch and French painting, Italian painting from the 15th to the 18th centuries, as well as French and Spanish painting from the Baroque period.

The sanctissimum – and most prized treasure – is Albrecht Dürer's Four Apostles of 1526, which came to Munich from Nuremberg thanks to a rather cunning move. Not to be missed are the other Old German Masters ranging from Altdorfer to Cranach on the upper floor, the 15th and 16th-century Italians, the Rubens Room, the 17th-century French paintings, Tiepolo's Adoration of the Kings and Jan Brueghel the Elder's Great Fish Market of 1603. Lovers of the Swabian School will find the wings of the altar from the Cistercian Abbey Church at Kaisheim, painted by Hans Holbein the Elder, on the ground floor.

Leo von Klenze, Ludwig I's famous court architect, incorporated several revolutionary architectural innovations when he designed the Alte Pinakothek at the beginning of the 19th century. He not only installed the first, visible, overhead windows in a museum but also introduced a completely new room layout conditioned by the intensity of natural light and the angle at which it enters the building. With his design, inspired by the Italian Renaissance, Klenze set a new standard for museum buildings throughout Europe. The lawns outside the museum have long since been a favourite picnic spot for the people of Munich. *Wed–Sun 10am–6pm, Tue 10am–8pm | entrance fee 7 euros, Sun 1 euro | Barer Str. 27 | www.pinakothek.de | U2 Theresienstraße, tram 27 Pinakotheken*

2 ENGLISCHER GARTEN ★
(131 D–F 1–6) (*⌀ J–M 6–1*)

This huge park is rightly called Munich's 'green lung' and can be put on a par with Central Park in New York and Hyde Park in London – or even above them. After all,

the 1000-acre English Garden is one of the largest urban parks in the world and many times the size of those mentioned above. From south to north it stretches for more than 5km (3mi) and is only crossed by the Isarring road near Kleinhesseloher See.

The Elector Karl Theodor, who had already opened the Hofgarten to the public, commissioned the military grounds to be remodelled to form a garden for the people so that not only his soldiers but also normal citizens could find somewhere to relax. His Army Minister, Sir Benjamin Thompson, later Count Rumford, who also made a name for himself as a physicist and inventor, came up with the necessary plan. Friedrich Ludwig von Sckell, a court gardener from Schwetzing, was commissioned with executing the project that at that time was unique in Europe. And, as the park grew steadily in size over the years, so did the population. In 1792, when the 'Theodor Park' as it was called

The lawns in the English Garden are just as popular with the local geese as sunbathers

to start with, was opened, 40,000 people were living in Munich.

The almost 78km (48mi) network of paths in Munich's 'green lung' can best be explored by bike. The most notable sights from south to north: right next to the Haus der Kunst, a chest-high wave formed in the *Eisbach* stream, just perfect for experienced surfers. This city-centre river-surfing location is even known in Australia. Just behind the Haus der Kunst is the *Japanisches Teehaus*. Regular INSIDER TIP traditional Japanese tea ceremonies and the Japanese Festival held on the 3rd Sunday in July, are highlights not only for those living in Munich. If you take the path towards the *Monopteros* (1836), designed by the architect Leo von Klenze, lots of nude sunbathers – for which the park is famous – can be seen to the left and right on the extensive ● grass areas. At the foot of the 'Mops', music from all corners of the world can be heard here when the weather is nice. At weekends

in particular, the grass areas are turned into a positiv open-air concert hall. Just a little bit further north, the beer garden at the *Chinesischer Turm* (1790), one of Munich's major landmarks, is the perfect place to quench your thirst and still your hunger. On the 3rd Sunday in July, the INSIDER TIP *Kocherlball*, a traditional folk dance, takes place here early in the morning *(6am–10am)*. In the olden days, this was where those working in large households could have some fun, as it was only early in the morning that they had any time to themselves.

At the top end of the southern section of the park is *Kleinhesseloher See* and the *Seehaus,* an up-market Bavarian café-restaurant, with a beer garden right next to the pond from where extremely romantic sunsets can be enjoyed. If you go through the underpass beneath the Mittlerer Ring road, you reach the northern section of the English Garden, at the far end of which is *Aumeister*. What is now a restaurant and beer garden was where the Master of the Royal Hunt used to live around 1810. There is also an ● amphitheatre with free performances in summer. *U3/6 Giselastraße or Universität*

3 GLYPTOTHEK (134 A1) *(⅏ H6)*
Munich's oldest museum: Ludwig I's famous collection of Antiquities opened its doors in 1830, predating even the British Museum or the Hermitage in St Petersburg. A perfect synthesis of form and content: one of Europe's most spectacular collections, housed in one of Germany's most important Classicist buildings. Most of the works on display, however, are copies. Designed by Leo von Klenze (1784–1864) in the style of an Ionic temple, the museum contains Greek and Roman sculptures dating from the 6th century BC to the 4th century AD. It is worth taking a look at all 13 exhibition rooms, concentrating perhaps on a few individual pieces. The most precious items in the museum's collection are, however, the well-preserved original pedimental sculptures from the Temple of Aphaea (500 BC) on the island of Aigina (Rooms VII and IX).

The inner courtyard of the Glyptothek conceals an idyllic refuge from the hustle and bustle of city life: a ● *café* beneath acacia trees surrounded by the vine-clad walls of the museum is the perfect place to daydream or to gather your own creative thoughts while have a cup of coffee and a delicious piece of cake. On Thu and Fri from July–Sept it acts as a backdrop for open-air plays. *Tue–Sun 10am–5pm, Thu 8pm | entrance fee 3.50 euros | Königsplatz 3 | www.antike-am-koenigsplatz.mwn.de | U2 Königsplatz*

4 KÖNIGSPLATZ (134 A1) *(⅏ G–H6)*
That the Acropolis in Athens provided the inspiration for this square is immediately obvious. The massive buildings rise like temples from Antiquity above the square. To make the effect of these light-coloured, shimmering buildings that much stronger, the architect used a few tricks. Königsplatz is not flat, but slopes slightly inwards from the buildings around the edge and over the grassed areas to the road that passes through the centre. This slight incline is enough to create the impression of ancient temple complexes that were always erected on hills. When Ludwig I commissioned a square to be laid out in the 19th century, it did not have to fulfil any specific purpose except that of copying the aesthetics of Ancient Greece. During the Nazi regime, Hitler had the square turned into a grey desert of stone, covering the grassed areas with massive granite slabs. It was not until 1988 that Königsplatz was returned – as far as possible – to its original appearance at the beginning of the 19th century. Today, a number of concerts and the *Kino Open Air* are held here every year. *U2 Königsplatz*

5 LENBACHHAUS (134 A1) *(⅏ G6)*
The home of the *Sammlung Blauer Reiter* (Blue Rider Collection) is closed until the end of 2013 for building work. Despite the general overhaul and construction of the new extension, the Kunstbau exhibition space on the mezzanine level in Königsplatz underground station, where temporary contemporary art exhibitions are held, remains open. *Kunstbau Tue–Sun 10am–6pm | entrance fee 8 euros | Luisenstr. 33/ Ecke Briennerstraße | www.lenbachhaus. de | U2 Königsplatz*

6 LEOPOLDSTRASSE
(130 C1–5) *(⅏ J4–5)*
Opinions about this road are divided as it is not particularly attractive. Lots of concrete, lots of traffic, all to do with appearances and not much substance. Until the early 1990s, Leopoldstraße was the

haunt of Munich's 'in' crowd. Apart from the Venezia ice cream parlour and Roxy, Café Extrablatt (1978–98) was the place to be in Schwabing. This was the beat of Germany's gossip columnists and where riotous parties were held for local celebrities. But these times are long gone. Nevertheless it's worth taking a stroll from the Siegestor (Triumphal Arch) up to Münchner Freiheit on a balmy summer evening. The boulevard is not only lined with countless artists proffering their wares but also cafés, pubs, fast-food outlets and restaurants, as well as boutiques, bookshops and discos. *U3/6 Giselastraße or Münchner Freiheit*

▣ LUDWIGSKIRCHE (130 C6) (*ⓜ J6*)

This neo-Romanesque Classicist church (by Gärtner) conceals a particularly valuable artefact: one of the largest frescos in the world (after Michelangelo's painting of the Sixtine Chapel), on the altar wall in the chancel, as well as The Last Judgement (by Peter Cornelius). The two towers are in direct contrast to the imposing Theatinerkirche to the south. *Ludwigstr. 20 | U3/6 Universität*

▣ LUDWIGSTRASSE
(134 C1) (*ⓜ J5–6*)

Walking up the monumental boulevard from the Feldherrnhalle at the southern end towards the Staatsbibliothek (State Library), the university and the Siegestor (Triumphal Arch), you get a clear impression of Klenze's plan to give Munich an opulent and grand thoroughfare, presenting a unified ensemble to show the world the might of the kingdom of Bavaria. *U3/6 Odeonsplatz or Universität*

▣ LUITPOLDPARK 130 B2–3) (*ⓜ H3*)

The people of Munich knew how to show their appreciation to their Prince Regent. On the occasion of his 90th birthday in

1911, the city presented Luitpold with 90 lime trees and planted them in a park which they named after him in the west

The Triumphal Arch at one end of Ludwigstraße balances the Field Marshals' Hall

of Schwabing. Today, the park is a much-loved recreational area. From here, it is just a short walk to the Olympic Park, passing *Bamberger Haus*, with its magnificent Baroque restaurant and Mediterranean flair, popular among both young and old. The frescos in the main hall on the first floor are also well worth seeing. *U2/3 Scheidplatz*

⑩ MÜNCHNER FREIHEIT
(130 C4) (⌖ J4)

Formerly known as Feilitzschplatz, this square was renamed after the war to commemorate members of the resistance who worked against Hitler's regime. A referendum in Schwabing held in 1998 led to the 'e' in 'Münchener' being omitted. Today, Münchner Freiheit is both a traffic intersection and the gateway to the north of Schwabing where things come alive at night around Occamstraße. The café *Münchner Freiheit* used to be popular meeting place for actors and a bronze statue of Helmut Fischer, who achieved cult status in Germany, now watches over the comings and goings. *U3/6 Münchner Freiheit*

⑪ MUSEUM BRANDHORST ★
(134 C1) (⌖ H6)

In May 2009, Munich's latest cultural attraction opened its doors to the public. An art museum that owes its existence to an unusual cooperation. The private collector Udo Brandhorst offered his collection to the Free State which constructed a building to house it. And what a building! The husband and wife team of architects, Matthias Sauerbruch and Louisa Hutton, made a façade out of 36,000 ceramic rods that gleam in 23 different colours and disperse light in such a way that you barely realise that the museum has any windows at all. Behind these is a second layer of folded and perforated sheet metal, that absorbs the noise of passing traffic. The ☺ museum building is one of the first devised with a sustainable ecological concept. More than 700 works of classical Modernist art are displayed on three levels, ranging from Joseph Beuys and Andy Warhol to Bruce Nauman. A whole storey is devoted to the painter and sculptor Cy Twombly. *Café Gaeta* or the lounge with a view of both Pinakothek museums are perfect places for a break. *Tue, Wed, Fri–Sun 10am–6pm, Thu 10am–8pm | entrance fee 7 euros | Theresienstr. 35 a | www.museum-brandhorst.de | U2 Theresienstraße, tram 27 Pinakothek*

The 'new' building housing the Neue Pinakothek was highly controversial 30 years ago

12 NEUE PINAKOTHEK
(134 B1) (*H6*)

As a counterpart to the Alte Pinakothek directly opposite, Ludwig I founded the Neue Pinakothek in the mid 19th century, but irreparable damage in the war resulted in the old Klenze building being demolished. Alexander von Branca's new building, opened in 1981 as the largest, new, post-war museum building in Germany, was greeted with a wave of enthusiasm but also critical discussion. Interest in the gallery, however, was and continues to be high, with its one millionth visitor passing through the door in the very first year after being opened. Some 550 paintings and 50 sculptures from the Rococo up to the Jugendstil period can be seen in 22 exhibition rooms. The principal focus, however, is on 19th-century European art from early Romantic painting, court painting under Ludwig I, the Nazarenes, French and German late Romantic painting and the Realists, to the 'German Roman' painters (von Marées, Böcklin, Feuerbach), the art of the Gründerzeit period and the French

Impressionists (Degas, Manet, Monet, Renoir). If 19th-century art is not to your taste, take a closer look at the early modern period: the Impressionists, Secessionists, Symbolists and Jugendstil. Temporary exhibitions are held on the lower floor. *Restaurant Hunsinger (closed Tue | www.restauranthunsinger.com)*, forming part of the museum building, boasts an international cuisine and seafood specialities. *Thu–Mon 10am–6pm, Wed 10am–8pm | entrance fee 7 euros, Sun 1 euro | Barer Str. 29 | north door | www.pinakothek.de | U2 Theresienstraße, tram 27 Pinakothek*

13 PINAKOTHEK DER MODERNE ★
(134 B1) (*H6*)

Brand new and yet already suffering from construction defects. From Feb–Sept 2013, the star attraction among Munich's art museums is going into exile. A structure called 'Die Schaustelle' to the southeast of the museum will act as a temporary but spectacular exhibition space. Admission is free. The idea behind the museum's original design was to provide an appropriate setting for four major state-owned collections and a number of private bequests under one roof. These include the State Gallery for Modern Art with works ranging from the Blue Rider to Beuys, and collections tracing the most important artistic developments in 20th and 21st-century painting, graphic works, design and architecture. The museum's light-filled wintergarden houses *Café Qivasou 48/8*, inviting visitors to take a welcome break. *Tue–Sun 10am–6pm, Thu 8pm | entrance fee 10 euros | Barer Str. 40 | www.pinakothek.de | U2 Theresienstraße, tram 27 Pinakothek*

14 STAATLICHES MUSEUM ÄGYPTISCHER KUNST
(126 B–C1) (*H6*)

Duke Albrecht V of Bavaria (1550–1579) acquired works of Egyptian art during his reign and now, 460 years later, the exhibits are being moved from the Residenz to the Kunstareal museum complex. The new, glass and concrete, subterranean State Museum of Egyptian Art (opening early 2013) covers 21,500ft² – three times its previous size. It enables the works – form all periods in Ancient Egyptian history up to the Coptic era – to be presented in an entirely new way. *Tue 9am–9pm, Wed–Fri 9am–5pm, Sat, Sun 10am–5pm | entrance fee 7 euros, Sun 1 euro | Gabelsbergerstr. 35 a | www.aegyptisches-museum-muenchen.de | U2 Königsplatz*

15 UNIVERSITÄT (130 C6) (*Ⓜ J5*)

The Ludwig-Maximilians-Universität, with its more than 45,000 students, is the second largest university in Germany after the Freie Universität Berlin. Names such

as Fraunhofer, Röntgen, Pettenkofer, Sauerbruch, Schelling, Riehl and Max Weber are synonymous with this seat of learning. The twin bowl-shaped fountains either side of Ludwigstraße are equally well-known. The university's address refers to the students Sophie and Hans Scholl who, as members of the 'White Rose' resistance group during the Hitler regime, were consequently executed in 1943. Outside the main building, the last leaflet distributed by the 'White Rose' movement can be seen carved in stone on the ground. *Geschwister-Scholl-Platz | U3/6 Universität*

GLOCKEN-BACH/AU/ HAIDHAUSEN

This fashionable district is a magnet for students, young designers and gays. Centred around Gärtnerplatz and the Glockenbach district (between the South Cemetery and the Isar), this is where life is led to the full. Whoever lives here is not only in tune with the times, but is more often than not a name in Munich's cultural, nightlife or gastronomic scene, and where you'll always be running into DJs, restaurateurs, club owners and models.

The Gründerzeit buildings in Hans-Sachs-Straße and the many little gardens are a reminder of the time when well-heeled entrepreneurs settled in this area. In the 1960s, this district was devoted to rock 'n roll and twist; now it's cocktail bars and clubs. Add to this the attractions of the Isar some of which, in Haidhausen, are on the right bank of the river. What could be nicer after a day in the Deutsches Museum than taking a dip in the Jugendstil swimming pool, the Müllersches Volksbad, or

Students take a break outside
Ludwig-Maximilians-Universität

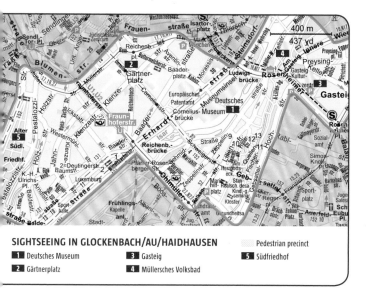

SIGHTSEEING IN GLOCKENBACH/AU/HAIDHAUSEN

1 Deutsches Museum **3** Gasteig **5** Südfriedhof

2 Gärtnerplatz **4** Müllersches Volksbad

▨ Pedestrian precinct

spending the evening listening to the city's best orchestra, the Munich Philharmonic, in the Gasteig cultural centre? In the meantime, the renaturalisation of the Isar has been completed. In the summer, the pebbly beaches, stone steps and small island between the Reichenbach and Wittelsbacher bridges are pretty crowded. The river is so clean, that you can leap into it without any hesitation.

1 DEUTSCHES MUSEUM ★ ●
(134 C3) *(ﾑ J8)*

Three weeks would probably not be sufficient to see everything in the Deutsches Museum. With 600,000ft² of exhibition space and some 28,000 objects, this is one of the largest science and technology museums in the world. The collection, begun in 1903 by Oskar von Miller, is constantly being added to. All the latest technological innovations can be found here, such as robots that can be seen working away in the Centre of New Technology, or

a reconstruction of the world's first wave power station located in Scotland. Special attractions include the space travel department, the mine in the basement, and the huge aviation and maritime exhibition halls. Some time should also be planned for a visit to the *Zeiss Planetarium (demonstrations 10am, noon, 2pm, 4pm | entrance fee 2 euros)*. In the *Sternwarte* (Observatory) you can take a look at the moon and Saturn every Tue and Fri at 9pm if the skies are cloud-free *(meet in the museum courtyard | free admission | www.beobachtergruppe.com)*. You can recover your strength in the restaurant or the cafeteria with free Internet access. Please note: the museum complex is being restored and will take 10–15 years. This means that certain exhibition areas will be closed from time to time. For more information, see the museum's website. *Daily 9am–5pm | entrance fee 8.50 euros | Museumsinsel 1 | www.deutschesmuseum.de | S-Bahn Isartor, tram 16 Deutsches Museum*

▣ GÄRTNERPLATZ ● (127 D6) (*Ø J8*)

This was Munich's first showcase 'square' laid out in a geometrical pattern in the 19th century, centred on a fountain and surrounded by flower beds. Even today, this circus opposite the Staatstheater am Gärtnerplatz (closed due to comprehensive restoration work until 2015), is one of the city's delights. Lots of cafés put tables out on the wide pavements when it's sunny. There is hardly a better place to soak up the comings and goings in this part of town. *U1/2 Fraunhoferstraße*

▣ GASTEIG (135 D3) (*Ø K8*)

When this red-brick building was completed in 1985, it was not well received by the general public who nicknamed it the 'culture bunker' as it did not fit into the architectural cityscape. In the meantime, the acoustics in the concert halls have made objectors change their tune and the Gasteig in Haidhausen has become one of the most successful cultural operations in Germany with around 750,000 visitors every year. You can often listen in on a number of the Munich Philharmonic Orchestra's rehearsals for next to nothing. This is also where the Munich Film Festival is held in June, when those in the international film business meet up. INSIDER TIP Free cinema tickets for open-air screenings in the inner courtyard are much sought after. *Rosenheimer Str. 5 | tel. 089 48 09 80 | www.gasteig. de | S-Bahn Rosenheimer Platz*

▣ INSIDER TIP MÜLLERSCHES VOLKSBAD ● (135 D3) (*Ø K8*)

The beautiful Jugendstil building was once Munich's first public indoor swimming pool. The vaulted ceilings above the two pools, the Roman/Irish steam bath with its open-air enclosure and the tiled saunas deserve an extended visit. *Daily 7.30am– 11pm | entrance fee from 3.70 euros, incl.* a 4-hour sauna 2.30pm | *Rosenheimer Str. 1 | www.swm.de | S-Bahn Rosenheimer Platz, tram 16 Deutsches Museum*

▣ INSIDER TIP SÜDFRIEDHOF (134 A–B 3–4) (*Ø G–H 8–9*)

A paradise for history fans. The South Cemetery was established in the 16th century as a burial ground for the poor. In the 17th century it accommodated the victims of the plague and, from the end of the 18th century onwards, it became Munich's main cemetery. Following its extension in the mid 19th century, it became the last resting place for many famous citizens, including the sculptor Roman Anton Boos (St Peter's), the architect Friedrich von Gärtner (Field Marshals' Hall), the historicist painter Wilhelm von Kaulbach, the architect Leo von Klenze and the painter of The Poor Poet, Carl Spitzweg. *Thalkirchner Str. 17 | U1/2/3/6 Sendlinger Tor*

NYMPHENBURG & NEUHAUSEN

Also known as 'Munich's other green lung', this district is dominated by the Baroque Schloss Nymphenburg. Vast swathes of grass, the palace canal and the splendid buildings of the former 'villa colony' lend this area a genteel air and have turned it into a popular place for the well-heeled people of Munich to withdraw to.

There is hardly a nicer place to go jogging than here, as Philipp Lahm – the FC Bayern and national team footballer – knows, as he grew up in the area. South of Rotkreuzplatz in Neuhausen things change – there is more traffic noise and many more shops. The *Wappenhaus* on Nymphenburger

Straße (recognisable by the coat-of-arms on its façade) once housed Munich's most expensive flat and was the setting of the popular 'Kir Royal' TV series.

■ BOTANISCHER GARTEN
(128 A4–5) (*ψ B4*)

The botanical garden that covers an area of just under 50 acres to the north of Nymphenburg Park, is one of the most beautiful in the whole of Europe – and that holds true all the year round. Aesthetics and science come together in perfect symbiosis here. The garden is a paradise for photographers and botanists. Whether in the formal garden, the genetics department, the Alpine House, the rhododendron grove or the arboretum, the splendour of nature unfurls before your eyes. From medicinal plants to carnivorous flowers the explanatory material on all the exhibits is informative without being scholarly. The terrace at the *Café Botanischer Garten*, located right in the middle of the complex, has a wonderful view of the rose garden. *Garden and café: Nov–Jan daily 9am–4.30pm, Feb/March/Oct 9am–5pm, April/Sept 9am–6pm, May–Aug 9am–7pm | entrance fee 5 euros | Menzinger Str. 65 | www.botmuc.de | tram 17, bus 143 Botanischer Garten*

■ HERZ-JESU-KIRCHE
(129 D5) (*ψ C5*)

After the old church burnt down in 1994, the architects Allmann, Sattler and Wappner designed the bold, shimmering blue glass structure of the new Church of the Sacred Heart in Neuhausen. At first, conservatively-minded residents were opposed to the new design, but it has since become a symbol of modern Catholic thought and is the venue for high-quality concerts and exhibitions. *Information: www.herzjesu-muenchen.de. Romanstr. 6 | U1 Rotkreuzplatz*

■ MUSEUM MENSCH UND NATUR
(128 A4) (*ψ B4*)

A light-hearted insight into natural history including the world of minerals, the history of life on earth and the 'problematic bear' bear Bruno – who caused quite a stir in the summer of 2006. He has now been stuffed and has his final resting place here. A INSIDER TIP free evening guided tour takes place every Thu. *Tue, Wed, Fri 9am–5pm, Thu 9am–8pm, Sat, Sun 10am–6pm | entrance fee 3 euros, Sun 1 euro | Nymphenburg Palace | www.musmn.de | tram 17, bus 51 Schloss Nymphenburg*

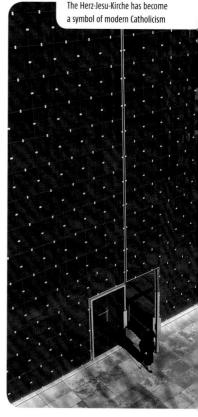

The Herz-Jesu-Kirche has become a symbol of modern Catholicism

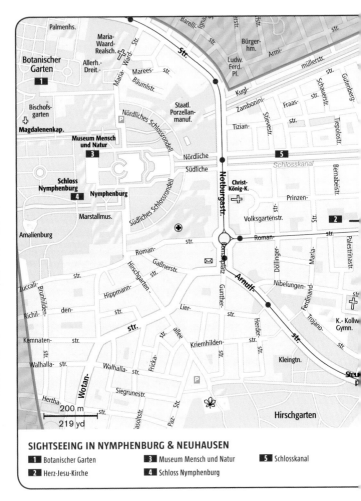

SIGHTSEEING IN NYMPHENBURG & NEUHAUSEN

1 Botanischer Garten
2 Herz-Jesu-Kirche
3 Museum Mensch und Natur
4 Schloss Nymphenburg
5 Schlosskanal

4 SCHLOSS NYMPHENBURG ★
(128 A5–6) (*ⓜ B4–5*)

Giving presents in the days of Elector Ferdinand Maria was done in style. In the mid 17th century his wife, Henriette Adelaide gave birth to a long-awaited son and heir, Max Emanuel. To honour his wife the proud father presented her with Nymphenburg Palace. The façade of this Baroque complex, built between 1664 and 1757, is around 700m long, three times that of the Oympic stadium. It was used by the ruling family of Bavaria as a summer residence and, walking through the magnificent apartments, you can imagine how elegant life must have been during the Golden Age of the Bavarian court.

Apart from the central building with its splendid Stone Hall and the Gallery of Beauties, the *Marstallmuseum* (Royal Stables) houses the world's most important collection of carriages, sledges and harnesses, and the *Porzellanmuseum* contains exquisite items from the Nymphenburg Porcelain Manufactory. Also worth a visit are the *Schlosspark* (palace garden) with its hothouses, the *Amalienburg*, a prime example of Rococo court architecture, the *Badenburg* with its Chinese wallpaper, the

⑤ SCHLOSSKANAL
(128 B–C5) (*ⓜ C–D 4–5*)

In Munich, all sorts of canals were planned in the 18th century which were to extend as far as Schleissheim Palace and Dachau Castle and would have enabled the Court to travel in comfort from one residence to the next by gondola. However, only this, the Palace Canal, was ever built. One of Munich's loveliest walks now runs alongside the absolutely straight canal towards Nymphenburg Palace. In summer, things

Nymphenburg Palace, formerly a summer residence, is also well worth visiting in winter

Pagodenburg with its chinoiserie, so fashionable at that time, and the *Magdalenenklause*, which Elector Max Emanuel had built in later life as a meditation chapel. *April–mid Oct daily 9am–6pm, mid Oct–March daily 10am–4pm | entrance fee for all attractions 11.50 euros | www.schloss-nymphenburg.de | tram 17, bus 51 Schloss Nymphenburg*

are quiet here, but in winter it can get very lively. As soon as the ice on the canal is thick enough, curling fans are out to enjoy their sport on more than 40 curling sheets – and carry on by flood-light until 10pm, with stalls selling mulled wine helping to keep everyone warm. Ice princesses and ice-hockey players also flit across the ice in Nymphenburg. *U1 Gern*

OTHER DISTRICTS

In Munich most things are focussed on the city centre. Districts such as Thalkirchen, with its lush green zoo, or the Olympic Park in the north of the city, are almost seen as being out of town, although they can easily be reached from the centre by public transport in just a few minutes.

Bavaria has its own Statue of Liberty too, on Theresienwiese

This actually explains one of the many advantages of the metropolis of Munich. Distances are always pretty short and travelling by public transport from one end of the city to the other never takes longer than an hour.

ALLIANZ ARENA ★ (0) (*0 0*)

Opened in May 2005, this temple to football is not only one of the most modern stadiums in the world, but has also developed into a top tourist attraction. When FC Bayern is playing, the stadium is lit up in red; when TSV 1860 kick off, it's a cool blue. Those interested in exploring the hidden corners of the stadium can even have a look into the teams' shower rooms on a guided tour. In the recently completed *FC Bayern Erlebniswelt (daily 10am–6pm | entrance fee 12 euros, children 6 euros | tel. 089 35 09 48)* you can relive the club's major successes in its more than 100-year history. It is a museum, film room, shop and meeting-place for fans all rolled into one. *Daily, except when there are matches, 11am, 1pm, 3pm, 4.30pm (Nov–March) or 5.30pm (April–Oct) | entrance fee 10 euros, tickets from the Allianz Arena Shop tel. (*) 01805 55 51 01, combined ticket Arena & Erlebniswelt 19 euros, tel. 089 350 94 83 50 | Werner-Heisenberg-Allee 25 (clearly visible from the A 9 Nuremberg motorway) | www.allianz-arena.de | U6 Fröttmaning*

BAVARIA/THERESIENWIESE ● ☀
(133 F3) (*0 F 7–8*)

Everybody in Munich and half of the world descend on the Theresienwiese every autumn for the Oktoberfest. What better place could the symbolic female figure of Bavaria have than on a slope above the Oktoberfest ground? Erected in 1850 by Ludwig I, the lady cast in iron by Ferdinand Miller guards the pantheon behind her in which famous Bavarians are honoured. When the 18m (60ft)-high statue was first constructed, it was considered a marvel of engineering. From the viewing platform inside Bavaria's head you have a unique view across to St Paul's church opposite. Marquees are not only put up here for the world's largest public festival but also for the 'Frühlingsfest' *(end of April)* and 'Winter-Tollwood' *(Dec)*. **INSIDER TIP** Bavaria's largest flea market is held here on the 1st Sunday of the 'Frühlingsfest'. *April–15 Oct daily 9am–6pm, during the Oktoberfest daily 9am–8pm | entrance fee 3 euros U4/5 Theresienwiese*

BAVARIA-FILMGELÄNDE ●
(137 D6) (*Ⅲ 0*)

Thanks to several major film productions and countless early-evening TV series, 'Hollywood-on-the-Isar' is – fortunately – still much in demand. Whether The Never-Ending Story, Das Boot (The Boat), Asterix and Obelix or The Baader Meinhof Complex, all these films have left their marks here that can be traced on a 90-min. tour. If you like, you can also book a 4-D cinema experience *(up until 4pm)* in addition. In summer, guided tours are held several times an hour; in winter on the hour. One of the highlights is the new **INSIDER TIP** Bullyversum – an interactive 3-D experience designed by Michael 'Bully' Herbig. *Daily 10am–3pm | entrance fee from 11 euros | Bavariafilmplatz 7 | www.bavaria-filmtour.de | tram 25 Bavariafilmplatz*

BMW-WELT/BMW-MUSEUM ★
(130 A2) (*Ⅲ G2*)

The BMW World located opposite the Olympia Park, an architectural masterpiece of glass and steel, is the Bavarian car manufacturer's brandname showcase and a venue for a variety of events. Guided tours *(from 7 euros)* focus on a variety of different subjects such as architecture, technology and the history of the traditional Bavarian car manufacturer. During this time, children (from 7 years of age) can explore the Junior Campus on their own and even take part in workshops. The BMW Museum, housing a large collection of vehicles and highlights from the company's history, is on the other side of the road. *BMW-Welt: daily 9am–6pm |*

Lerchenauer Str. 57 | www.bmw-welt.com | U3 Olympiazentrum; BMW-Museum: Tue–Sun 10am–6pm | entrance fee 12 euros | Am Olympiapark 2 | www.bmw-museum.de | U3 Olympiazentrum

The Aviation Museum in Schleissheim is a branch of the Deutsches Museum

DEUTSCHES MUSEUM FLUGWERFT SCHLEISSHEIM (0) (*Ⅲ 0*)

The Aviation Museum, which forms part of the Deutsches Museum, was opened on a historical site in Oberschleissheim in 1992. The aerodrome and its buildings were built in 1912–19 for the Königlich-Bayerische Fliegertruppen (Royal Bavarian Flying Battalion). The evolution of flight can be traced from Otto Lilienthal's glider contraption from the early days of aviation to jump jets and helicopters, even including a 30m (98ft)-high rocket from 1971. You can take to the skies yourself in a flight simulator. *Daily 9am–5pm | entrance fee 6 euros | Effnerstr. 18 | Oberschleissheim | www.deutsches-museum.de | S-Bahn Oberschleissheim*

FLAUCHER ●/ FLOSSLÄNDE THALKIRCHEN

(136 C4) (*ᗄ F–G 10–12*)

The 'Flaucher' stretches along the river banks of the Isar between Brudermühl and Tierpark bridges. When the weather is nice, the area is teeming not only with sunbathers but also barbecue enthusiasts. In summer, the night sky is lit up by hundreds of campfires along the beaches. A little bit further south is Flosslände where Thalkirchen campsite can be found. This is also another INSIDER TIP river-surfing hotspot. Both beginners and experienced surfers come here as it is no where nearly as dangerous as on the Eisbach. *U3 Thalkirchen, bus 135 Thalkirchen Campingplatz*

KZ-GEDENKSTÄTTE DACHAU

(138 C3) (*ᗄ 0*)

Just a few weeks after Adolf Hitler was appointed Reichskanzler, a concentration camp 'for political prisoners' was established in Dachau, 20km (12½mi) from Munich, which became a prototype for all other concentration camps that followed. Today, an exhibition documenting the site's history can be seen in the former barracks as well as the cell blocks, the two crematoriums and a reconstruction of the prisoners' barracks. The memorial site provides an oppressive and very realistic insight into the darkest chapter in Germany's history. *Tue–Sun 9am–5pm | free admission | Alte Römerstr. 75 | www.kz-gedenkstaette-dachau.de | S2 Dachau*

MAXIMILIANEUM (135 D2) (*ᗄ K7*)

In the exuberant spirit of the 19th century, Maximilian II wanted to erect a genuine 'Acropolis' at the end of Maximilianstraße. The architect Friedrich Bürklein fulfilled his wish in 1876. Originally intended to provide accommodation and teaching facilities for exceptionally gifted students in Bavaria (the foundation still exists and provides free board and lodging to selected students who achieve the top grade, 1.0, in their Abitur), the Bavarian Parliament and the Senate of the Free State moved into the building in 1949. By law, any citizen may sit in on public sessions, but visitors are advised to phone in advance to find out the times of guided tours. *Tel. 089 4 12 60 | www.bayern.landtag.de | U4/5 Max-Weber-Platz*

OLYMPIAGELÄNDE

(129 E–F 2–3) (*ᗄ F–G 2–3*)

Munich's Olympic site and park) has become world-famous for its revolutionary, contemporary architecture. When the city was selected to hold the Summer Games in 1972, the local authorities set about spreading the Games' motto, 'The Happy Games', even while the sports complex was still under construction. The architectural practice Behnisch and Partner reworked the archaic tent construction principle and erected a daring string of roof structures, each one being an entity in its own right, on the 740 acre site formerly used as a royal military training ground at Oberwiesenfeld, dwarfed by the 291m (955ft)-high ★ ☼ *Olympiaturm (Olympic Tower) (entrance fee 4.50 euros)*. Lifts operate 9am–midnight. The first stop is at a height of 181m (594ft), where the award-winning chef, Otto Koch, runs a gourmet restaurant focussing on international cuisine. Just 9m (30ft) above the revolving restaurant *181 (→ p. 65)*, is the tower's viewing platform. Music fans will want to visit the INSIDER TIP *Rockmuseum (free admission | www.rockmuseum.de)* which houses a myriad of collectors' items. The centre of the Olympic complex is the *stadium* which accommodates 80,000 spectators. This is where Munich's two football clubs (FC Bayern und TSV 1860) used to play before the Allianz Arena was built in 2005. 50m further on is the

INSIDER TIP *Olympiaberg* (Olympic Hill). Just below the summit is Munich's highest beer garden at 564m (1850ft) above sea level, the *Olympia Alm (daily | www.olympiaalm.de)*. The 2-hour guided ☂ tour of the tented roof construction is certainly one of the park's highlights *(April–Nov | from 39 euros | tel. 089 30 67 24 14)*. ● Free pop concerts take place during the summer in the Theatron by the Olympic Lake. Those who want to listen to anecdotes about well-known figures in the world of sport, can hire an MP3 player *(April–Oct from the information kiosk in the ice rink complex, Nov–March in the Olympiaturm | price: 7 euros | deposit: 50 euros)*.

Tucked away in the southern part of the park is the die *Ost-West-Friedenskirche*. This 'church of peace' was created by the Russian hermit 'Väterchen Timofei' in the 1950s from rubble salvaged from buildings destroyed in the war. Today, this unusual church is a museum *(daily 10am–4pm | Spiridon-Louis-Ring 100). www.olympiapark.de | U3, bus 173 Olympiazentrum*

VILLA STUCK (135 E2) (*🕮 K7*)

The neo-Classicist Jugendstil villa of the 'princely painter' Franz von Stuck is located in the heart of Munich's exclusive district of Bogenhausen. The artist's home, completed in 1898, was the glittering focal point of social life during his lifetime. On the ground floor, the representative reception rooms with their opulent wall decorations can be viewed, as well as Stuck's collection of paintings, sculptures and furniture. Upstairs is his former studio, finished like a banqueting hall with a coffered ceiling, beautiful Gobelin tapestries and the Altar to Sin. *Tue–Sun 11am–6pm | entrance fee 4–9 euros | Prinzregentenstr. 60 | www.villastuck.de | U4 Prinzregentenplatz, tram 16 Friedensengel/Villa Stuck*

The Villa Stuck is an idiosyncratic work of art both inside and out

FOOD & DRINK

Bavarian cooking isn't just *Leberkäs* (meatloaf) and *Weißwurst* (white sausage), *Schweinsbraten* (roast pork) and *Knödel* (dumplings), as delicious as these may be. It is much more varied, sophisticated – and even more individual – than most people think.

The mixture of different cooking styles that the 'wild young' chefs in the top-end sector propagate, may seem odd to some. But be bold and plump for a creation that may even sound dubious! Of course, if you prefer to play safe, you can always rely on the firmly established Asian, French and Italian culinary perfection to be found in Munich. But despite the international lean,

local specialities ranging from Kalbsbries (sweatbread) to Saure Lüngerl (marinated lung) are always tempting. And thanks to the exceptional quality of the water in Bavaria's lakes, fish is plentiful. Whitefish from Lake Starnberg and trout from the Aumühle fish farm in the Isar valley are duly famous.

One tip when browsing through a menu: if it says Schweinebraten instead of Schweinsbraten, then the restaurant is probably not typically Bavarian. Where Kalbsmedaillon und pommes de terre (veal medallions with potatoes) are served, you'll be paying a lot of money for something that is definitely not Munich fare.

Photo: White sausages and a pretzel

Whether hearty food without any frills, creative fusion cooking or refined haute cuisine – Munich has something to everyone's taste

Munich's waiters and waitresses, or at least those in the 'genuine' Bavarian restaurants, are often rather gruff. You should add up to 10% as a tip, or at least round up the amount charged.

BEER GARDENS

Almost all beer gardens close at 11pm and, unless it says otherwise, they are all open every day, except when it's raining or the temperature is lower than 13°C (55°F). A unique feature of beer gardens is that you can bring your own food and have a picnic, regardless of how big or small the beer-garden is. Drinks, on the other hand, have to be bought at the outdoor bar. This however only applies to those areas of the garden where there is no waitress service.

Idyllic beer garden next to Kleinhesseloher Pond in the English Garden

AUGUSTINERKELLER (133 E1) (🗺 F6)

Legendary for its Stammtisch (table reserved for regulars) around which many a famous local character has been seated. This is where the culture of the traditional beer garden with its freshly tapped cool beer (from a wooden barrel) is nurtured. *Arnulfstr. 52 | tel. 089 59 43 93 | www.augustinerkeller.de | S-Bahn and tram 16, 17 Hackerbrücke*

CHINESISCHER TURM ● (131 D6) (🗺 K5)

The Chinese Tower is where both punks and the famous come to enjoy their Hofbräu beer. On Wed from 4pm, Sat from 1pm and Sun from noon a band plays in the tower. *Englischer Garten 3 | tel. 089 3 83 87 30 | www.chinaturm.de | U3/6 Gisela-straße, bus 54/154 Chinesischer Turm*

HOFBRÄUKELLER (135 D3) (🗺 K7)

A peaceful oasis above the Isar. At least until offices close when it gets pretty crowded as it also attracts masses of young party-goers, drawn by the Mexican beach bar. *Innere Wiener Str. 19 | tel. 089 4 59 92 50 | www.hofbraeukeller.de | U4/5 Max-Weber-Platz*

KÖNIGLICHER HIRSCHGARTEN (128 B6) (🗺 C6)

You have to wash up your own stein in this, Bavaria's largest beer garden. The Augustiner beer comes straight from the barrel and a fallow deer enclosure is a reminder of the former royal hunting tradition. *Hirschgarten 1 | tel. 089 17 99 91 19 | www.hirschgarten.de | tram 17/16 Steubenplatz, bus 51 Hirschgartenallee*

LÖWENBRÄUKELLER (129 F6) (🗺 G6)

Home of the brewery of the same name that has been here since 1883. It's almost always party-time at Christian Schottenhamel's regardless of whether at the 'Starkbierfest' (bock beer festival), Fasching (carnival), a summer festival or in the intimate beer garden. *Nymphenburger Str. 2 | tel. 089 54 72 66 90 | www.loewenbraeu keller.com | U1, tram 20/21 Stiglmaierplatz*

SEEHAUS (131 D4) (*ω K4*)

See and be seen. Despite all the people-gazing, the lovely beer garden right next to Kleinhesseloher Pond is *en vogue* all year round. *Kleinhesselohe 3 | tel. 089 3 81 61 30 | www.kuffler-gastronomie.de | U3/6 Münchner Freiheit*

WALDWIRTSCHAFT (136 B6) (*ω 0*)

This is where the beer garden protest against early closing times started in 1995. Thanks to the successful revolt, beer gardens can now stay open once again until 11pm. The 'WaWi', as it is generally called, is also known for its INSIDERTIP live jazz and blues concerts and its idyllic location high above the Isar gorge just beyond the city boundary. *Georg-Kalb-Str. 3 | Großhesselohe | tel. 089 74 99 40 30 | www.waldwirtschaft.de | S7 Großhesselohe and then a 15-min. walk*

CAFÉS

AROMA KAFFEEBAR (126 B6) (*ω H8*)

There's only seating for 20 with standing-room for the same number. But this mini-café epitomises the charm of the Glockenbach district. Having got a place, you then have to decide between an array of home-blended coffees and home-made cakes and salads. *Daily | Pestalozzistraße 24 | U1/2/3/6 Sendlinger Tor*

CAFÉ AM BEETHOVENPLATZ (133 F3) (*ω G8*)

Chopin and chocolate gâteau, Mozart and mozzarella. Here you can eat well, enjoy a few drinks and be looked after by attentive student-style service. *Daily | Goethestr. 51 | U3/6 Goetheplatz*

INSIDERTIP CAFÉ FRISCHHUT (123 D6) (*f H7*)

Locals call the café on Viktualienmarkt 'Die Schmalznudel' – as it is rightfully famous for its delicious, deep-fried dough speciality – *Schmalzgebäck* – prepared in front of your eyes and served with a cup of strong coffee. For those with a bigger appetite there is also a selection of savoury snacks. *Closed Sun | Prälat-Zistl-Str. 8 | U/S Marienplatz*

CAFÉ GLOCKENSPIEL ⚞ (127 D4) (*ω H7*)

Meeting place for the 'in' crowd with the best view of Marienplatz and a heated roof terrace. Way-out drinks! *Daily | Marienplatz 28 | U/S-Bahn Marienplatz*

JOSEFA (133 E2) (*ω F7*)

'Alva's choc dream' and a café au lait – what a perfect afternoon. Located between the Transport Museum, Theresienwiese and the main station, this little, charming

---

MARCO POLO HIGHLIGHTS

★ **Marais**
Charming café and shop in booming Westend → p. 64

★ **Tramin**
Munich's high flyer, reaching for the Michelin stars → p. 64

★ **Makassar**
Mediterranean cuisine fused with Creole → p. 65

★ **Mangostin**
Asian mix meets Bavarian beer garden tradition → p. 67

★ **Daylesford Organic**
Organic eatery and shop in a lovely old building → p. 69

★ **Fraunhofer**
Excellent food with no-frills in this traditional hostelry → p. 69

CAFÉS

café is a good place to come to. Sometimes there are also short live concerts. *Daily | Westendstr. 29 | www.josefa.eu | tram 18/19 Holzapfelstraße* ·

MARAIS ★ (133 E2) (ℳ F7)

Tasteful shop and café in Westend. The breakfasts and snacks are popular with the arty crowd. The shop also sells furniture, accessories, jewellery, children's things and cosmetics. *Closed Mon | Parkstr. 2 | www.cafe-marais.de | tram 18/19 Holzapfelstr.*

CAFÉ REITSCHULE ☺

(131 D5) (ℳ K5)

Elaborately renovated in 2009, the café-restaurant dating from 1927 now shines again in its former glory. What hasn't changed is the view through large windows of the university's indoor riding school. Importance is laid on using local produce; pancakes with home-made jam are also served at breakfast. *Daily | Königinstr. 34 | www.cafe-reitschule.de | U3/6 Giselastraße*

GOURMET RESTAURANTS

Acquarello (135 E2) (ℳ M6)

Famous for its refined Italian 'country' cooking and truffles. One of the best contemporary Italian restaurants in the city. When you get to the dolci, you'll certainly wish you had room for more. Set menu from 69 euros. *Daily | Mühlbaurstr. 36 | tel. 089 4 70 48 48 | www.acquarello.com | U4 Böhmerwaldplatz*

Emiko (127 D5) (ℳ J7)

This up-market restaurant in the Louis Hotel on the Viktualienmarkt doesn't only serve sushi but also Japanese haute cuisine and delicacies such as the famous Wagyu steak (50 euros). *Daily | Viktualienmarkt 6 | tel. 089 41 11 90 81 11 | www.louis-hotel.com | U/S-Bahn Marienplatz*

Schuhbecks in den Südtiroler Stuben (127 E4) (ℳ J7)

Star chef Alfons Schuhbeck conjures up his delicious dishes, famous throughout Germany, using regional produce. 5-course dinner, incl. drinks: 145 euros. *Closed Sun | Platzl 6 and 8 | tel. 089 2 16 69 00 | U/S-Bahn Marienplatz*

Schweiger² (134 C3) (ℳ J8)

Exquisite crossover cuisine in bright surroundings. Thanks to their informal manner, the professional TV chef Andreas Schweiger and his wife Franziska turn a 3–9-course dinner of your choice (from 90 euros) into an unforgettable experience. *Closed Sat, Sun | Lilienstr. 6 | tel. 089 44 42 90 82 | www.schweiger2.de | S-Bahn Rosenheimer Platz*

Tantris (131 D3) (ℳ J3)

Munich's longest-standing, star-studded restaurant. Superb cooking. Evening dinner from 140 euros (5 courses) *Closed Sun, Mon | Johann-Fichte-Str. 7 | tel. 089 3 61 95 90 | www.tantris.de | bus 54, 144 Parsivalplatz*

Tramin ★ ☺ (135 D4) (ℳ K8)

Understated décor and furnishings; the food and wines are anything but understated. Choice compositions using mostly local produce, just perfect for the ecologically minded. Set menu from 55 euros. *Closed Sun, Mon | Lothringer Str. 7 | tel. 089 45 45 40 90 | www.tramin-restaurant.de | S-Bahn Rosenheimer PLatz*

TAMBOSI ● 〜 (127 E2) (*ω J6*)

One place you can guarantee sitting in the sun, both in winter (with rugs) and in summer (with thick sunglasses). Tambosi is popular with tourists after a walk around the Court Garden and with the locals who like to see and be seen. *Daily | Odeonsplatz 18 | www.tambosi.de | U3/4/5/6 Odeonsplatz*

TIZIAN (126 C3) (*ω H7*)

Café restaurant that is busy at midday, for afternoon coffee and after work. Centrally located but tucked away in a courtyard. The décor and furnishings, with its moulded plaster ceiling and golden picture frames, is rather reminiscent of turn-of-the-century coffeehouses. In summer, you can enjoy a piece of cake and a cappuccino on the terrace around the large fountain. *Daily | Maxburgstr. 4 | U/S-Bahn Karlsplatz (Stachus)*

A guarantee for a gourmet cuisine without the pomp: the Schweigers

RESTAURANTS: EXPENSIVE

181 (129 F3) (*ω F2*)

A culinary experience in the clouds – the city's highest location. The restaurant is divided into two categories: Business and First Class. Located 181m (594ft) above ground level. Not only the panorama over the city is breath-taking: the perfectly arranged creations by the award-winning chef, Otto Koch (Koch = Cook – nomen est omen), are also a feast for the eye – before the tastebuds take over. *Daily | Spiridon-Louis-Ring 7 | tel. 089 3 50 94 81 81 | www.restaurant181.com | U3 Olympiazentrum*

KLEINSCHMIDTZ (134 B3) (*ω H8*)

There is barely a good-food guide that doesn't go into raptures about the skills of the chef at Kleinschmidtz. The set menu (3 or 4 courses) in particular is always good for one or other culinary surprise. And those who don't feel pecky can enjoy a glass or two in an informal atmosphere in the wine bar. *Daily | Fraunhoferstr. 13 | tel. 089 2 60 85 18 | www.kleinschmidtz.de | U1/2 Fraunhoferstraße*

KÜNSTLERHAUS (126 B3) (*ω H7*)

Fascinating view of the hustle and bustle on Lenbachplatz and expertly prepared specialities from the grill on the first floor of this time-honoured artists' meeting house. Although not exactly cheap, the Wagyu rumpsteak and Charolais fillet are worth every penny. *Closed Sun | Lenbachplatz 8 | tel. 089 45 20 59 50 | www.kuenstlerhaus-gastronomie.de | U/S-Bahn Karlsplatz (Stachus)*

MAKASSAR ★ (134 A5) (*ω G9*)

Mediterranean, French and colonial specialities in the Dreimühlen district. The head chef was once the cook on board the marine explorer Jacques Cousteau's ship, and has a way with hot, spicy Creole dishes. His crème brûlée is a real favourite. Please note: no credit cards accepted. *Closed Sun | Dreimühlenstr. 25 | tel. 089 77 69 59 | www.*

The food is prepared before your eyes in the pillared restaurant Brenner

makassar.de | bus 152 Ehrengutstraße, bus 131 Röcklplatz

NEKTAR (135 D3) (*ɷ K8*)

The snow-white restaurant with its loungers that first opened in 2003, has already become a firm favourite. Nektar is such an irresistible place: you can enjoy a dinner of several courses – inspired by the crossover cuisine's book of tricks – while reclining, entertained by performances in between and a tasteful mixture of sounds from the DJ. Barbecue fans go into raptures about the **INSIDER TIP** grill in a vaulted cellar. *Closed Sun, Mon | Stubenvollstr. 1 | tel. 089 45 91 13 11 | www.nektar.de | tram 16 Gasteig*

TRADER VIC'S (127 D3) (*ɷ H7*)

South Sea specialities in the cellar of the Bayerischer Hof. A helping of barbecued suckling pig and a Menehune cocktail and the illusion of being so far away is perfect. It was from here that the Mai Tai took the cocktail scene in Germany by storm in the 1970s. *Daily | Promenadeplatz 2–6 | tel. 089 2 12 09 95 | www.bayerischerhof.de | U/S-Bahn Marienplatz*

RESTAURANTS: MODERATE

ANH-THU (130 B5) (*ɷ H5*)

Vietnamese delicacies in red and gold surroundings with, unfortunately, rather too many seats for the space. But top marks for the very friendly service and fresh ingredients for the totally authentic dishes. Reservation absolutely essential. *Daily | Kurfürstenstraße 31 | tel. 089 27 37 41 17 | www.anh-thu.de | tram 27 Nordendstraße/ Elisabethplatz*

BRENNER ☺ (127 E3) (*ɷ J7*)

The restaurant, divided into three sections (bar, pasta kitchen, grill) in this listed pillared hall, is definitely the cosiest location in the otherwise rather sterile Maximilianhöfe. The food is mostly organic, the fish fantastic. The best place to sit is near the wood-fired oven. *Daily | Maximilianstr. 15 | tel. 089 4 52 28 80 | www.brennergrill.de | tram 19 Kammerspiele*

LE FLORIDA (130 B5) (*ɷ H5*)

Interesting food combinations such as goats' cheese and sliced apple, served in pleasantly subdued lighting. The curry dishes (tam tams) are legendary in Munich. *Daily | Georgenstr. 48 | tel. 089 44 42 95 55 | www.leflorida.de | tram 27 Nordendstraße*

KRANZ ☺ (134 B3) (*ɷ H8*)

Organic cuisine of the highest order. The menu varies depending on the season and regional produce available. The home and hand-made pasta is a real delight. The interior décor is as exquisite as in a 1-star restaurant. *Daily | Hans-Sachs-Str. 12 | tel. 089 21 66 82 50 | www.daskranz.de | U1/2/3/6 Sendlinger Tor, tram 16, 17, 18 Müllerstraße*

MANGOSTIN ★ (136 C2) (*ɷ F12*)

A beer garden with an unusual Asian touch. Outside, wan-tan soup is served under the chestnut trees; inside there are Japanese and Thai restaurants as well as a cocktail bar. A bit off the beaten track (but ideal after a visit to the zoo), Mangostin has become a firm fixture among Munich's gourmet crowd. *Daily | Maria-Einsiedel-Str. 2 | tel. 089 7 23 20 31 | www.mangostin.de | U3 Thalkirchen*

MONSIEUR HU (134 A4) (*ɷ G9*)

Architecturally a highlight, especially the 'light tunnel' in the middle section where you can dine if you book correspondingly early. The food ranges from Vietnamese to Cantonese. Good soups and meat skewers to barbecue yourself. The main courses could sometimes do with a bit more umph. *Daily | Dreimühlenstr. 11 | tel. 089 45 21 72 72 | www.monsieurhu.de | U3 Poccia-straße, bus 152 Ehrengutstraße*

INSIDER TIP NO MI YA
(135 D3) (*ɷ K8*)

An unconventional mixture that, for years, has ensured the restaurant is fully booked. As No Wed Ya is more a little tavern than a big Japanese restaurant, the food is Bavarian Japanese. The Japanese staff and the Bavarian manager serve Unertl wheat beer to schnitzel-sushi, udon soup und yaki-tori. *Daily | Wörthstr. 7 | tel. 089 4 48 40 95 | www.nomiya.de | U4/5 Max-Weber-Platz*

ROSSINI (133 F5) (*ɷ J5*)

Ten years after Helmut Dietl's film of the same name appeared on the big screen, the real-life Rossini opened its doors in Munich – even with the original sign over the entrance. Inside, indulge in quality Italian cuisine and enjoy the genuine atmosphere of the cinema classic. *Closed Sun | Türkenstr. 76 | tel. 089 33 09 42 70 | www.ristoranterossini.net | U3/6 Universität*

SALT (133 F1) (*ɷ G6*)

Tastefully furnished restaurant over two floors near the main station with ambitious international cooking and well-trained staff. You can put together a meal of your choice in the evenings. *Closed Sun | Rundfunkplatz 4 | tel. 089 89 08 36 95 | www.saltrestaurant.de | U/S-Bahn Hauptbahnhof*

No Mi Ya: Japanese food in a traditional Bavarian setting

LOCAL SPECIALITIES

▶ **Aufgschmalzene Brotsuppe** – originally considered a poor man's meal, now to be found on up-market regional menus. Pieces of bread soaked in stock are fried and served with the soup.

▶ **Ausgezogene** – a deep-fried sweet 'pastry' varying in circumference from 4½ to 8in. Traditionally made at harvest thanksgiving and for major church holidays. Nowadays, the 'Kirchweihnudel' is made by every baker.

▶ **Böfflamott** – like many things in Bavaria, this comes from the French (originally bœuf à la mode). Ox meat is braised with two calves' hooves for four hours.

▶ **Knödel** – few Bavarian dishes do without the good old dumpling. Whether Brezen, Semmel, Kartoffel, Leber or Zwetschgenknödel (pretzel, bread(roll), potato, liver or prune dumplings), the homemade ones are the best, served for example with chanterelles in a cream sauce.

▶ **Leberkäs** – meatloaf in a bread roll is one of the survival tactics of those in a hurry. It doesn't contain either liver or cheese (as the name would suggest) but a secret concoction of beef, pork and lots more, too.

▶ **Obatzda** – 'batz' means a clod or lump of earth. Obatzda however is mature Camembert mixed into a thick paste with butter, onions, spices and a drop of beer (photo top right).

▶ **Saures Lüngerl** – a lung ragout cooked in a sour stock and served with a cream sauce and bread dumplings.

▶ **Schlachtschüssel** – boiled meat, black pudding and liver sausage, pork belly and sauerkraut: once a firm favourite that was only served the day the animals were slaughtered. Nowadays it has rather sunk into oblivion.

▶ **Schweinsbraten** – roast pork seasoned with salt, pepper and ground caraway seeds and with diamond-shaped crackling. Roasted with quartered onions and basted with a dark wheat beer. Usually served with dumplings. Beware of restaurants offering 'Schweinebraten' – the true Bavarian dish is spelt 'Schweinsbraten' (photo top left)!

SCHMOCK (130 A6) *(ᗰ G6)*

The proprietors have discovered a niche in the market and serve an international range of Israeli/Arabic food in this wonderful old building together with kosher to costly wine and cocktails. The meat is sourced from kosher butchers. *Daily | Augustenstr. 52 | tel. 089 52 35 05 35 | www. schmock-muenchen.de | U2 Theresienstraße*

SPATENHAUS AN DER OPER 🌿 (128 E3) *(ᗰ J7)*

Traditional but sophisticated Bavarian cooking. From both rooms on the first floor and from the terrace there is an excellent view to be had of the Opera House and Max-Joseph-Platz. *Daily | Residenzstr. 12 | tel. 089 2 90 70 60 | www. kuffer-gastronomie.de | tram 19 National-theater, U/S-Bahn Marienplatz*

VINORANT ALTER HOF (127 E4) *(ᗰ J7)*

The walls of what used to be an imperial fortress built by Ludwig the Bavarian in the 13th century, now house a Franconian wine bar and restaurant. Beyond the bar (with finger-food) are the 'Galgenkeller' (Gallows' Cellar) and the 'Einsäulensaal' (One-Pillar Hall), all of which serve excellent food, especially delicacies from northern Bavaria. INSIDER TIP 'Dinner in the Dark' (Wed–Sun) is a 4-course set menu served in complete darkness. *Daily | Alter Hof 3 | tel. 089 24 24 37 33 | www.alter-hof-muenchen.de | U/S-Bahn Marienplatz*

DAYLESFORD ORGANIC ★ ☺ (127 E4) *(ᗰ J7)*

Heaven for fans of ecologically correct and sustainable natural products and food. You can either buy meals to take away in this organic delicatessen or eat in the café-cum-shop. INSIDER TIP Dinner served until 11pm. *Closed Sun | Ledererstr. 3 | tel. 089 45 20 98 33 | www.daylesford organic.de | U/S-Bahn Marienplatz*

The frikadellers in the Spatenhaus are still made like in the good old days

ZUM DÜRNBRÄU (127 E4) *(ᗰ J7)*

An alternative to the Hofbräuhaus and located right next door. In this inn that has been here for 500 years, you have to squeeze close together but that means you get to know the others at the table (who are frequently not local) that much more quickly. The roast pork and dumplings served in a spicy dark sauce is unbeatable. *Daily | Dürnbräugasse 2 | tel. 089 22 21 95 | S-Bahn Isartor*

FRAUNHOFER ★ (126 C6) *(ᗰ H8)*

Munich's trendy eatery is popular with both old and young, the 'in' crowd and families. On Sundays you get a free lesson in Bavarian culture as the traditional morning pint is always accompanied by music. If you're not very hungry, try the lard and onion spread on bread or meat-loaf with home-made potato salad. The theatre of the same name and studio cinema are both part of the set-up. *Daily | Fraunhoferstr. 9 | tel. 089 26 64 60 | www.fraunhoferwirtshaus.de | U1/2 Fraunhoferstraße*

The Hofbräuhaus also has a traditional beer garden

INSIDER TIP▶ GASTSTÄTTE GROSSMARKTHALLE ●
(133 F5) (*∅ G 9*)
For lovers of true Bavarian cooking. This is where those working in the wholesale market normally eat – and that's why it's open already at 7am and closes at 5pm (Sat at 2pm). This is where you'll find the very best Weißwurst there is. And the roast pork isn't too bad either. *Closed Sun | Kochelseestraße 13 | tel. 089 76 45 31 | www.gaststätte-grossmarkthalle.de | U3/6 Implerstraße, bus 131 Gotzinger Platz*

HOFBRÄUHAUS (127 E4) (*∅ J7*)
The Hofbräuhaus is so well known that it's no surprise it's full of hordes of tourists from the USA, Asia and Italy. Those who prefer a bit more peace and quiet can sit in the lovely beer garden in the courtyard in summer and in the Bräustüberl upstairs in winter. *Daily | Platzl 9 | tel. 089 2 90 13 60 | www.hofbraeuhaus.de | U/S-Bahn Marienplatz*

INSIDER TIP▶ MAO (130 A5) (*∅ G5*)
One of Munich's loveliest Chinese restaurants – modern and (thanks to the long wooden tables) a very sociable place. Tip: Langlebenssuppe ('longevity soup') with Chinese medicinal herbs and beef. *Daily | Schleissheimer Straße 92 | tel. 089 54 35 67 12 | www.mao-muenchen.de | U2 Josephsplatz, bus 154 Görresstraße*

OCUI (126 C5) (*∅ H7*)
The name is an abbreviation of 'open cuisine' – where you can look over the chefs' shoulder. But you also have to be your own waiter and head back to your table after waiting a few minutes with a full tray. Everything here revolves around pizzas, pasta and Asian dishes that are prepared before your eyes and to your own individual wishes. *Daily | Oberanger 31–33 | tel. 089 54 22 60 01 | www.ocui.de | U1/2/3/6 Sendlinger Tor*

PRINZ MYSHKIN ☺ (126 C4) (*∅ H7*)
The wonderful high vaulted ceiling of the former beer store and the huge windows lend Munich's best vegetarian restaurant

a cosmopolitan flair. Massively popular, so reserve a table well in advance. *Daily | Hackenstr. 2 | tel. 089 26 55 96 | www.prinzmyshkin.com | U/S-Bahn Marienplatz*

RUFFINI ☺ (129 D5) (𝄞 E4)

Quality at a fair price. Café and winery, shop and cooperative. This is where the established artist has breakfast next to the radio DJ. In summer, everybody can enjoy the tiny roof terrace. *Closed Mon | Orffstr. 22–24 | tel. 089 16 11 60 | www.ruffini.de | U1 Rotkreuzplatz*

LA TAZZA D'ORO (130 C5) (𝄞 J4)

This Italian bar in the heart of Schwabing's chaotic shopping district has prices that are well below what is typical in this area. Its made-on-the-spot pasta is magical. Lively atmosphere in the evening – three cheers! *Closed Sun | Hohenzollernstr. 13 | tel. 089 33 38 37 | U3/6 Giselastraße*

WEISSES BRÄUHAUS (127 E4) (𝄞 J7)

A good old Bavarian hostelry with blunt, grumpy but surprisingly efficient waitresses who serve the most divine bread dumplings on earth. Despite all things traditional, they also keep up with the times here and have a Bräuhaus app for iPhones. *Daily | Tal 7 | tel. 089 2 90 13 80 | www.weisses-brauhaus.de | U/S-Bahn Marienplatz*

VINOTHEQUES

WALTER & BENJAMIN
(127 D5) (𝄞 H8)

Fine wines from the best-known vineyards with accompanying specialist literature to match. A small but exquisite selection of food is also served *(Tue–Sat evenings, Fri, Sat also at lunchtime)*. *Closed Sun | Rumfordstraße 1 | tel. 089 26 02 41 74 | www.walterundbenjamin.de | tram 16/18 Reichenbachplatz*

GARIBALDI BAR (130 B6) (𝄞 H5)

Wine and food, with an emphasis on Italy, at fair prices. The wine shop of the same name, where you can order larger quantities, is right next door. *Daily | Schellingstr. 60 | tel. 089 28 67 36 70 | www.garibaldibar.de | U3/6 Universität*

GEISEL'S VINOTHEK (134 A2) (𝄞 G7)

More than 500 quality wines in the wine cellar and excellent food from the kitchen. A few yards down the road, right next to the Hotel Königshof, is the *Weingalerie* shop *((126 B3) (𝄞 H7) | Karlsplatz 25)* that enjoys an excellent reputation not just among sommeliers and wine aficionados. *Daily | Schützenstr. 11 | tel. 089 55 13 70 | www.excelsior-hotel.de/restaurants/geiselsvinothek | U/S-Bahn Hauptbahnhof*

LOW BUDGET

▶ The money-strapped with a taste for good food head for *Alter Simpl* where few dishes cost more than 10 euros. *Daily |* **(130 C6)** *(𝄞 H5) | Türkenstr. 57 | tel. 089 2 72 30 83 | www.eggerlokale.de | U3/6 Universität*

▶ *Gute-Nacht-Wurst* actually serves genuine Berlin curry sausages with tasty sauces and Bavarian beer. *Daily |* **(127 D6)** *(𝄞 H8) | Klenzestraße 32 | tel. 089 80 06 97 83 | www.gute-nacht-wurst.de | U1/2 Fraunhoferstraße*

▶ A cheap alternative for fans of Asian food. No dish costs more than 10 euros in *Jasmin*. *Daily |* **(133 E4)** *(𝄞 F9) | Lindwurmstr. 167 | tel. 089 76 77 57 | www.jasmin-asia-cuisine.de | U3/6 Poccistraße*

SHOPPING

CITY WHERE TO START?

Neuhauser and **Kaufingerstr. (127–128 B–D 3–4)** *(🗺 H7)*, with all the high street names, Oberpollinger department store and the Hypo-vereinsbank and Kaufinger Tor arcade and its delicatessens run between Stachus and Marienplatz (U/S-Bahn Karlsplatz (Stachus), Marienplatz). **Theatiner** and **Maximilianstraße (127 D–F 2–4)** *(🗺 J6–7)* are both home to luxury labels, designer boutiques and shopping arcades such as the Fünf Höfe.

As in other areas, Munich offers a huge variety when it comes to shopping as well, ranging from the cosmopolitan and exclusive, to the traditional and unusual. And everybody has their own favourite district too. Those who like everything close together on just a few streets, as in many other metropolises around the world, should concentrate on the city centre, on and around Marienplatz.

Department stores, clothes shops and jewellers all jostle for space. But street artists and buskers still manage to catch shoppers' attention, even if only for a short while, as they rush from one store to another. Those after international luxury

Photo: The Fünf Höfe and Salvatorpassage

Fashionable brands, luxury labels, young designers and traditional costumes: whatever you're looking for, you'll find it here

labels will find what they're looking for under one roof near Stachus: urban life-style products can be found on three floors in Oberpollinger, disguised as a top-quality department store. This traditional address was given a comprehensive workover by the London-based architects Virgil & Stone to create a glamorous premier department store to compete with the elegant bou-tiques on Maximilianstraße and attract both well-heeled locals and wealthy tour-ists from Japan and the Far East.

The other axis of the pedestrian precinct runs from Marienplatz to Odeonsplatz and is more for those with a 'fatter wallet'. In ★ *Theatinerstraße,* in the architectur-ally interesting *Fünf Höfe* and in the other attractive arcades that branch off to both sides, exquisite fashion boutiques, gen-tlemen's outfitters, milliners, Italian shoe-shops, jewellers and art galleries can be found. This exclusive shopping district takes in the whole of the area around Perusastraße and Residenzstraße right up as far as Briennerstraße and Salvatorplatz. The ★ *Gärtnerplatz* district used to be

Sams & Son: an eldorado for collectors and those who love traditional bags and cases

the gay area; now it is (also) a shopping paradise for fans of more exotic fashions. This is where you'll find hemp clothing as well as daringly innovative haute couture studios. Bored taggers-on can be parked in one of the many cafés or sent to the hairdressers – this district seems to have the highest density of *coiffeurs* anywhere in the world. But Munich's uncontested luxury shopping boulevard has to be *Maximilianstraße*. Between the National Theater and the Old Town ring road you'll only find the most expensive there is to

be had – whether you're into hunting gear, jewellery or art.

In the past few years, *Sendlinger Straße*, from Marienplatz to Sendlinger Tor, has developed into an attractive shopping street with a number of small boutiques with affordable prices. Near Asamkirche is the *Asampassage*, an oasis right in the middle of the city with cafés, bars and shops. The street running from Marienplatz to Isartor is called *Tal* with everything from souvenir shops and Bavarian kitsch for tourists, to computer shops.

Those looking for more avant-garde and way-out things have to head for Schwabing, to the student district between *Leopold-straße, Hohenzollernstraße, Amalienstraße, Schellingstraße* and *Türkenstraße*. Fashions and fashion stores come and go quickly here: just wander around, have a look and let yourself be inspired. Those in search of designers, innovative store concepts and small creative cells far from pedestrian precincts and well-trodden tourist routes should head for *Haidhausen (U4/5 Max-Weber-Platz)* and *Westend (U4/5 Schwan-thalerhöhe)*. While wandering around these areas you'll come across some unusual places as well as some uncon-ventional window dressing and slogans. Shops and department stores in the city centre are open from Mon–Sat 9am–8pm (in the rest of the city most are open only until 6pm and on Sat until 2pm).

ANTIQUES

Antique shops are centred on Schwabing's Türkenstraße, Barerstraße and Brienner-straße, around Promenadeplatz and in the side streets between Isartor and Fraunhoferstraße.

CURTIS & CURTIS (135 D3) (*⑩ K7*)
This family business has specialised in antique dining tables in particular and

the famous Thonet chairs, but also makes beautiful solid wood furniture to measure in the 19th-century style in its own workshop. Old model planes, rocking horses and antique porcelain make a short detour worthwhile. *Wiener Platz 8 | www.curtisundcurtis.de | U4/5 Max-Weber-Platz, tram 18 Wiener Platz*

RECYCLE ART (134 B5) (ℳ J9)

On trips throughout Europe, antique furniture and unusual home accessories are bought and then restored with considerable care and attention to detail before being offered for sale again. Just take a seat at the coffeebar in the shop and gaze at the range of goods on offer. *Closed Mon | Humboldtstr. 27 | www.recycle-art.de | U1/2 Kolumbusplatz*

INSIDER TIP SAMS & SON
(134 B3) (ℳ H8)

For set decorators, fans of oldtimers and collectors this is a top address as the small shop is packed to the ceiling with antique furniture, trunks, wardrobe trunks and globes. The historical croc-cases from the 1930s from Rosenheim in Berlin are a special treat. *Mon–Fri 1pm–7pm, Sat 11am–2pm | Fraunhoferstr. 23 | www.alte-koffer.de | U1/2 Fraunhoferstraße*

DELICATESSEN

DALLMAYR ★
(127 D4) (ℳ J7)

Munich's traditional and stylish delicatessen. In the historical food halls with their marble columns, a paradisiacal array of delicacies awaits the gourmet: fresh salads, paté, lobster and salmon, a selection of 120 different types of sausage and cold meat, 250 varieties of cheese, game, poultry and meat. Not to mention fine blends of tea and coffee, wines, exclusive tobacco, a marvellous confectionery department, exotic specialities and an exclusive pasta section. On the first floor is the shop's own restaurant. *Dienerstr. 14/15 | www.dallmayr.de | U/S-Bahn Marienplatz*

★ **Theatinerstraße**
Exquisite – applies to both the shops and the architecture
→ p. 73

★ **Gärtnerplatz district**
Munich's creative scene peoples the cafés and hairdressing salons
→ p. 74

★ **Dallmayr**
Delightful traditional, classy delicatessen with a gourmet restaurant
→ p. 75

★ **Ludwig Beck**
The department store full of special ideas
→ p. 76

★ **Susanne Bommer**
Minimalistic design from Munich with an Asian touch → p. 80

★ **Fünf Höfe**
Munich lifestyle meets international shopping flair → p. 79

★ **Maximilianhöfe**
Cool shopping temple
→ p. 79

★ **Viktualienmarkt**
Fresh market produce in the ultimate of traditional Munich settings
→ p. 79

★ **Iki M.**
Munich's hippest organic fashion space shows how to be environmentally and ethically correctly dressed → p. 80

★ **Eduard Meier**
Germany's oldest shoeshop has been around for more than 400 years → p. 81

MARCO POLO HIGHLIGHTS

DEPARTMENT STORES

(126 B6) (*ⓜ H8*)

High-quality, delicious products with a blessing from above: vinegars and oils, wild garlic spread and herbal teas, tagliatelle and Schweinsöhrl biscuits produced in monasteries. Tip: a small hamper makes

Expensive but breakable: carefully crafted Nymphenburg porcelain

a lovely present. *Pestalozzistr. 16 | www.genesis-feinkost.de | U1/2/3/6 Sendlinger Tor*

KÄFER (135 E2) (*ⓜ L7*)

Local celebrities can be seen from time to time in this hip delicatessen. The focus of its comprehensive range of fare is on fish, wine and cheese (350 different types). Käfer attracts customers with its alternating Italian and French weeks. Also famous for its tent at the Oktoberfest and its large outlet markets in Parsdorf, Brunnthal and Pullach. *Prinzregentenstraße 73 | www.feinkost-kaefer.de | U4 Prinzregentenplatz*

DEPARTMENT STORES

BASIC ☺

Munich's first organic store is a real winner. Top locations, top-quality produce from certified sources, an atmosphere that's a far fling from the Jesus-sandled crowd, and an excellent snack bar have made 'all things green' a trendsetter. *www.basic-bio-genuss-fuer-alle.de* (127 E4) (*ⓜ J7*) | *Westenriederstr. 35 | U/S-Bahn Marienplatz* (130 A4) (*ⓜ G4*) | *Schleissheimer Straße 158–62 | U2 Hohenzollernplatz* (129 E6) (*ⓜ F6*) | *Nymphenburger Str. 82 | U1 Mailingerstraße* (135 F1) (*ⓜ M6*) | *Richard-Strauß-Str. 48 | U4 Böhmerwaldplatz*

HIRMER (126 C4) (*ⓜ H7*)

The largest men's outfitters in the world near the Frauenkirche stretches over six floors. Up-market labels such as Ralph Lauren, Boss, Calvin Klein and Burberry can be found here of course as well as the company's own tailoring service. Discerning customers will find what they are looking for on the lower level; *loft.28* on the first floor is aimed as the younger streetwear generation. *Kaufingerstr. 28 | www.hirmer-muenchen.de | U/S-Bahn Marienplatz*

LUDWIG BECK ★ ● (127 D4) (*ⓜ J7*)

The store with a difference: individual, up-beat and with its very own charm. Arranged over six floors, Becks sells popular, quality and traditional clothes as well as items by young designers. It also has a vast stocking, sock and button department. The selection and offers in the CD section for, jazz, ethnic and classical music is unique. Beck's music department where stars often hold autograph sessions, received a special ECHO award in 2008 for its exceptional and modern presentation in the classical music sector. *Marienplatz 11 | U/S-Bahn Marienplatz*

ART

The best-known galleries are to be found in and around Maximilianstraße. Every first Thursday in the month is late-night opening.

INSIDER TIP DINA4 PROJEKTE
(130 A6) (*ᗒ H5*)

Innovative gallery full of ideas. Instead of being displayed in an internal exhibition space, works by artists waiting to be dis-covered are hung in the shop windows. *Wed–Fri 1pm–6pm, Sat noon–4pm | Theresienstr. 51 | www.dina4projekte.de | U2 Theresienstraße*

GALERIE F5,6 (127 E1) (*ᗒ J6*)

The spotlight here is on photography. Apart from works by established photographers, there are also pictures by younger, more experimentally-minded artists at lower prices. Those just wanting to look can gain inspiration from one of the temporary exhibitions. *Tue–Fri noon–6pm, Sat noon–5pm | Ludwigstr. 7 | www.f5komma6.de | U3/6 Odeonsplatz*

LOTHRINGER13 (135 D4) (*ᗒ K8*)

A Munich art institution to which the *Städtische Kunsthalle Munich, Spiegel* and the exhibition space *lothringer13/laden* belong. Well-established avant-garde gal-lery over 8600ft² with a new exhibition every 6 weeks. The emphasis is on media art. *Tue–Sun 2pm–8pm | Lothringer Str. 13 | www.lothringer13.de | S-Bahn Rosenheimer Platz*

ARTS & CRAFTS

NYMPHENBURGER PORZELLAN
(127 E2) (*ᗒ J6*)

The prices at Bavaria's famous, high-qual-ity porcelain manufactory are way beyond what most people would spend on a normal shopping spree. The shop exudes an air of exclusivity and tradition (since 1747). *Odeonsplatz 1 | www.nymphenburg. com | U3/6 Odeonsplatz*

INSIDER TIP VIER WERKSTÄTTEN
(134 D3) (*ᗒ H8*)

Most of the products in this brightly-lit shop are from regional craftspeople and designers and include paper objects made by the proprietor, felt shoes, bags made of bicycle tubes, ceramics and jew-ellery. *Fraunhoferstr. 20 | U1 Fraunhofer-straße*

LOW BUDGET

▶ Everyone will find the dirndl or lederhose they need for the Oktoberfest at *Wies'n Tracht & mehr* at rock-bottom prices; from short to long, pink to dark blue. **(127 E4)** (*ᗒ J7*) | *Tal 19 | www.wiesn-tracht-mehr.de | U/S-Bahn Marienplatz*

▶ Hugo Boss suits for a fraction of their original price can be found at *Gerdismann.* **(126 C6)** (*ᗒ H8*) | *Fraunhoferstr. 9 | www.gerdismann. de | U1/2 Fraunhoferstraße*

▶ Choose something fitting for the evening from all the elegant period clothes and dinner jackets at *Kaktus-blüte.* **(127 E5)** (*ᗒ J8*) | *Rumfordstr. 26 | www.die-kaktusbluete.de | S-Bahn Isartor*

▶ You can find Dior, Chanel and Yves St. Laurent at bargain prices at *Alexas Retrofashion.* **(127 D5)** (*ᗒ H/J 7s*) | *Utzschneiderstr. 10 | www.alexas.de | U/S-Bahn Marienplatz*

WACHSZIEHER AM DOM
(127 D4) (*ω H7*)

Specialist candle shop, also selling wax pictures. Franz Fürst, the master chandler, is one of the few non-industrial candle-makers left and is happy to answer questions. *Thiereckstr. 2 | www.kerzen-fuerst. de | U/S-Bahn Marienplatz*

MARKETS & FLEA MARKETS

Munich has hardly anything to offer flea-market fans any more. You can still find a few bits and bobs at lunchtimes during the week around the *Unimensa* (university canteen) in Giselastraße (130 C5) (*ω J5*). Bavaria's flea market that covers the largest area, on the *Messegelände* in München Riem (138 C3) (*ω S7*), is also popular. *(Fri/Sat, when no trade fair is being held | U2 Messestadt-Ost).*

FARMERS' MARKETS

The only weekly market in Munich selling exclusively organic produce is in ☺ Perlach. Meat and sausages from cattle and pigs allowed to roam and graze freely, milk from happy cows and free-range eggs *(Sat 7am–1pm | (138 C3) (ω N11) |*

Pfanzeltplatz | U2 Karl-Preis-Platz, bus 55 Pfanzeltplatz).

Self-caterers may well want to visit the *markets in the Au district (Wed, Sat 8am–1pm) | (134 C4) (ω J8–9) | Mariahilfplatz | bus 52/152 Mariahilfplatz)* and in *Neuhausen (Thu 10am–7pm |* (129 D6) *(ω E5) | Rotkreuzplatz | U1 Rotkreuzplatz).*

ELISABETHMARKT
(128 B5) (*ω H4–5*)

Small and intimate. Few tourists stray to this corner of Schwabing. The market on Elisabethplatz is a treasured remnant of life as it used to be in Old Schwabing. Fruit, vegetables, cheese, fish, poultry and flowers are on sale. The **INSIDER TIP** ☺ Biokäsemanufaktur (stand 19) has a wide range of organic cheeses, wine and eggs. You must try the sourdough bread! *Mon–Sat | Elisabethplatz | tram 27 Elisabethplatz*

FLOHPALAST (130 B6) (*ω G5*)

Hunt and rummage for bargains under cover, protected from the wind: this flea market is in a shop where standholders rent shelf space. The range of goods includes CDs, DVDs, jewellery, antiques and clothing. Well worth a visit. *Theresienstr. 81 | www.flohpalast.de | U2 Theresienstraße*

RELAX & ENJOY

The ● *Olympiabad* with a sauna landscape covering 9600ft² fulfills (virtually) every wish. Listen to the twitter of birds and other natural sounds as well as the 'Aqua Viva', a coloured light and sound simulation, while relaxing in the *sanarium* – or treat yourself to a massage. *Mon 10am–11pm, Tue–Sun 8am–11pm | sauna day pass 21.50 euros | (129 F3) (ω F3) | Coubertinplatz 1 | tel.*

089 23 61 50 50 | U3 Olympiazentrum Yoga to combat tired muscles and for a relaxed but active mind. Anyone can take part – even complete beginners – in the free, 45-min. ● *Yoga classes* that are held in summer in the open in the middle of Westpark. *May–Sept Sun 9.30am | (132 B5) (ω E9) | Westpark, entrance Pressburger/Reulandstraße | www.sport-muenchen.de | U6 Westpark*

VIKTUALIENMARKT ★
(127 D5) (*Ⓜ J7*)

The largest and oldest food market in Munich (established in 1807), just a stone's throw from Marienplatz, has kept something of its much praised intimacy and atmosphere and offers high quality at equally high prices. The stallholders, some of whom are real characters, sell fruit, vegetables, herbs, flowers, milk products, eggs, poultry, wine, bread and honey.

the 'Five Courtyards' project. This shopping arcade and bar complex can well be compared to its bigger competitors in New York or Paris. The city's zest for life can be felt here in condensed form: from the bookshop to luxury boutiques, fine glass to an art gallery – the Hypokunsthalle – and Schumann's daytime bistro to the Barista restaurant. *Between Theatinerstraße and Kardinal-Faulhaber-Straße | www.fuenfhoefe.de | U3/6 Odeonsplatz*

Balsam for the senses: a fruit stand on Viktualienmarkt

Fish and venison are in the market halls; the butchers have their own row of stands in the arcades below St Peter's. *Mon–Sat | U/S-Bahn Marienplatz*

SHOPPING ARCADES & CENTRES

FÜNF HÖFE ★ ● (128 D3) (*Ⓜ H–J7*)

Herzog and de Meuron, who designed the Allianz Arena, were also involved in

MAXIMILIANHÖFE ★
(127 E–F3) (*Ⓜ J7*)

This luxury shopping complex matches up well to international competition from other similar meccas. Brand names include Etro, Versace, Dolce & Gabbana, Chopard, as well as jewellers and the exclusive children's clothing label Valentina & Me. The atmosphere behind Bürklein's magnificent 19th-century façade is a bit on the cool side due to the steel and glass construction inserted in the grand shell. *Maximilianstr. 11–15 | www.maximilian-hoefe.de | tram 19 Kammerspiele*

OBERPOLLINGER (126 B3) (*ᗯ H7*)

One of the best and most modern, award-winning department stores in Europe, this 3-storeyed shopping oasis near Stachus is home to international luxury labels from A for Aigner to Z for Zoeppritz. The 'Premium Beauty' department on the ground floor, with brand names such as Mac, Hermès, Gucci, SBT, Prada, Tom Ford, Versace and John Varvatos, is remarkable. A quick drink at the Veuve Clicquot Champagne bar is part and parcel of the up-market shopping experience! *Neuhauser Str. 18 | www.oberpollinger.de | U/S-Bahn Karlsplatz (Stachus)*

FASHION & ACCESSORIES

For many years Munich has been a city that the fashion world has looked to – and not just for traditional clothing. Since 2010, a fashion week has been held for hip designers – several of whom are based in Munich such as Gabriele Blachnik (*(127 F3) (ᗯ J7) | Marstallstr. 8 | www.gabriele-blachnik.de | tram 19 Kammerspiele*), Lola Paltinger (*(127 E4) (ᗯ J7) | Tal 27 | www.lolapaltinger.com | U/S-Bahn Marienplatz*) and Talbot Runhof (*(127 D6) (ᗯ H8) | Klenzestr. 41 | www.talbotrunhof.com | U1/2 Fraunhoferstraße*) as well as Marcel Ostertag (*(134 B4) (ᗯ H8) | Westermühlstraße 3 | U1/2 Fraunhoferstraße*) and Michael Wagner (*(134 B3) (ᗯ H8) | Fraunhoferstr. 4 | U1/2 Fraunhoferstraße*), who already enjoy international success.

SUSANNE BOMMER ★
(127 D5) (*ᗯ H–J7*)

Her first shop was in Haidhausen, now she's in the Gärtnerplatz district. The Munich designer Susanne Bommer is known for her unfusy, often plain-coloured and always wearable fashions. Due to their clear cut and colouring they sometimes have an Asian touch. *Rumfordstr. 4 | www.susannebommer.de | tram 16/18 Reichenbachplatz*

DOPPLER
(135 D3) (*ᗯ K8*)

If you're in the Haidhausen area you should drop in here. This lovely shop has lots of unusual little accessories from from charm bracelets to bags. *Metzstr. 15/ entrance Sedanstraße | www.doppler-shop.de | S-Bahn Rosenheimer Platz*

ERTLRENZ
(134 C3) (*ᗯ J8*)

Sports shop run by experts: Sven Renz was an active German triathlete, his wife Martina Ertl-Renz has more than 15 years experience as a world champion Olympic skier. The staff are equally passionate runner and skiers. *Brienner Straße 13 | www.ertlrenz.de | U3/4/5/6 Odeonsplatz*

INSIDER TIP ▶ HANNIBAL MENSWEAR
(126 C6) (*ᗯ H8*)

This still very young menswear label is named after its owner: Simon Hannibal Fischer. It stands for puristic design with an emphasis on suits and streetwear with a touch of the avant-garde. *Holzstr. 11 | www.hannibal-collection.com | U3/6 Sendlinger Tor*

IKI M. ★ ☺
(127 E4) (*ᗯ J7*)

Organic can be beautiful too! At Iki M. you'll only find clothes made by environmentally approved companies that back fair working conditions. 'Green' labels include Kuyichi, Katharine Hamnett and Edun. *Marienstraße 6 | www.iki-m.de | S-Bahn Isartor*

ROECKL
(126 C4) (*\mathcal{M} H7*)

A traditional company that has been making high-quality gloves since 1839. Once you cross the threshold you'll be fascinated by the appeal of such exquisite products. And the sales staff can judge your glove size just at a glance. Other accessories include scarves and caps. *Sendlinger Str. 1, Maffeistr. 1 | www.roeckl.com | U/S-Bahn Marienplatz*

ROOM TO ROAM ☺
(135 D3) (*\mathcal{M} K7*)

Organic fashion for the younger generation. This label places value on individual designs and styles that are compatible with the ecologically correct, fair-trade fashion philosophy: full of surprise, refreshing, tantalising, flexible. The designer Akela Stoklas and her team merge creativity with the bold and inquisitive. *Johannisplatz 21 | www.roomtoroam.de | U4/5 Max-Weber-Platz*

SERVUS HEIMAT
(126 C4) (*\mathcal{M} H7*)

Bavaria is the centre of the universe – or that's what the locals think anyway. And for all those who don't believe it, take a look at this through-and-through Bavarian clothes shop. You'll soon change your mind, confronted with all those t-shirts, tops and bags with local motifs. *Brunnstraße 3 | www.servusheimat.de | U1/2/3/6 Sendlinger Tor*

SHOES

EDUARD MEIER ★
(127 E3) (*\mathcal{M} J7*)

Germany's oldest shoeshop – purveyors to the Court since 1596. On the visiting cards it says: 'Fine Shoes, Hunting Suits, Fly Fishing'. You can even attend a shoe-cleaning seminar – good leather needs

looking after and the boss himself gives talks on the rights and wrongs of shoe care. *Residenzstr. 22 | www.edmeier.de | U3/4/5/6 Odeonsplatz*

Barbie dolls in traditional costume at Servus Heimat

HALFS ● (130 B6) (*\mathcal{M} K4*)

Makers of the best Haferlschuhe (traditional brogues) in Munich. What was once worn by hunters and miners is now an absolute must for every serious Oktoberfest visitor. And for those who prefer something a little more with-it: Achim Wünsch also has a number of sporty or elegant variations on the theme. *Closed Mon | Feilitzschstr. 35 | www.halfs.de | U3/6 Münchner Freiheit*

INSIDER TIP HEELS ANGELS
(127 E6) (*\mathcal{M} H8*)

Women know that you only find the perfect shoe once. That's why Heels Angels make exact copies of that treasured but worn-out object of desire. Beautiful, handmade one-offs also available, including extravagant clogs, fantastic high-heels and chic leather handbags. *Klenzestr. 45 | www.heels-angels.de | U1/2 Fraunhoferstraße*

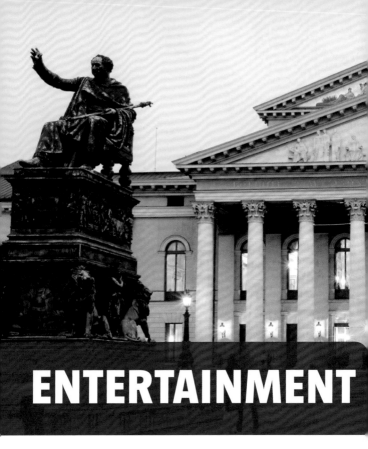

ENTERTAINMENT

CITY WHERE TO START?
The easily walkable stretch Müllerstraße – Sonnenstraße – Maximiliansplatz (126 B–C2–6) (*⚏ H6–8*) (U1/2/3/6 Sendlinger Tor) is perfect for an evening stroll and to find out more about Munich's nightlife. Dozens of venues for all tastes are located here and in the side streets. The gay scene is in and around Müllerstraße, whereas the young crowd head for the area around Stachus at the northern end of Sonnenstraße.

'A village of a million inhabitants' or a metropolis? Not an easy question to answer. Munich does have a colourful selection of bars, clubs, discos, cinemas and late-night dives, but for a proper subculture the situation is a bit difficult. The last remaining underground dens have been luxuriously renovated and red tape make things more conservative than cooperative.

If you do a little homework beforehand to see what is going on and where, have enough stamina (to deal with the bouncers), are adventurous enough (you never really know what, why and when something is 'in') and have got cash to spare,

Photo: The Nationaltheater

Munich shines – especially at night. The Bavarian capital offers culture and nightlife to suit every taste

you won't find it hard to have fun until the early hours. The most popular places for going out are Gärtnerplatz and the Glockenbach district (new venues opening every month, mainly for the 'in' crowd), Schwabing (for the slightly older, lots of tourists), Haidhausen (lots of cocktail bars, Westend (up-and-coming, alternative) and Maxvorstadt (student crowd).

BARS

CAFÉ AM HOCHHAUS (126 C6) (*ꔮ H8*) Formerly a café for grannies, with wild wallpaper, huge picture windows, interesting non-mainstream DJs and a generally euphoric, worked-up atmosphere. A fixed star between Gärtnerplatz and the Glockenbach district. *Daily | Blumenstr. 29 | www. cafeamhochhaus.de | U1/2 Fraunhoferstraße*

Schumann's: excellent cocktails in a classic bar setting

local DJs at the turntables. *Closed Sun | Müllerstr. 31 | www.ksar-barclub.de | U1/2/3/6 Sendlinger Tor*

MAURO'S NEGRONI CLUB
(133 D3) (*M K8*)

Stylish offshoot of Negroni, on the next parallel road, with classic, dark wood panelling. Good Italian food meets the Campari embassador Mauro Mahjoub's expertly mixed cocktails. **INSIDER TIP** Live jazz concerts and DJ evenings once a month. *Daily | Kellerstr. 32 | www.negroni-club.de | S-Bahn Rosenheimer Platz*

SCHUMANN'S (127 E2) (*M J6*)

Even if many mourn the loss of the bar on Maximilianstraße, Charles Schumann feels very much at home in the Hofgarten. Fans of gimlets and roast-beef freaks have got used to the new venue and keep on coming to Germany's best-known bar-keeper. During the day, you can enjoy a drink in the adjoining bar, *Camparino*, and lunch until 3pm *(closed Sat, Sun)*. *Daily | Odeonsplatz 6–7 | www.schumanns.de | U3/4/5/6 Odeonsplatz*

VEGA (130 C5) (*M H5*)

Despite the name, the screen hero Vincent Vega hasn't been spotted here, but that doesn't bother the slightly older cinema fan who finds the crowd in other bars too young. Noticeably high percentage of women, friendly barkeepers and the DJs play mostly older-style funk, soul and Indie pop music. *Closed Sun, Mon | Georgenstr. 56 | www.vega-bar.de | tram 27 Nordendstraße*

DISCOS

INSIDER TIP ELLI DISCO
(126 A3) (*M G7*)

In the disco era in the '70s and '80s, Munich was a producer's bastion. Elli

INSIDER TIP BAR CENTRALE
(127 E4) (*M J7*)

Close to the Hofbräuhaus and yet a world away – at least with regard to the atmosphere. Italian bar with the charm of well-worn furniture, Campari and a yearning for the sea. Snacks at lunchtime and in the evenings, and usually packed to the gills as far back as the rear lounge. *Daily | Ledererstr. 23 | www.bar-centrale.com | U/S-Bahn Marienplatz*

KSAR (126 C6) (*M H8*)

Still one of Munich's best 'in' places in an excellent location. The picture windows look out onto the lively Glockenbach district. Sit back and enjoy a Mai Tai, perfectly shaken and mixed at the bar. Excellent house music with well-known

Disco is a musical follow-up to the 'Sound of Munich' of old with an unobtrusive LED light show projected on the ceiling. The club is dimly lit, labyrinthine and intimate; the public outwardly flirty. Great fun. *Closed Sun–Wed | Elisenstr. 35 | www.ellidisco.de | U/S-Bahn Hauptbahnhof*

KULTFABRIK (135 E4) (*W L9*)

The former Kunstpark Ost site was often doomed to die in the hands of property sharks but licencees have fought back successfully. Last orders won't be until 2015 now. Some 20 bars and clubs jockey for the favour of a young crowd from the Munich area. On Fridays, a good dozen venues club together and open their doors for a 5 euro flat rate. *Daily | Grafinger Straße 6 | www.kultfabrik.info | U/S-Bahn Ostbahnhof*

MAXIMILIANSPLATZ
(126 C2–3) (*W H6–7*)

A conglomeration of party haunts can be found to the north of Stachus, within walking distance of Sonnenstraße. 5 clubs alone are housed in a former insurance building at Maximiliansplatz 5. The best-known is the Munich branch of the disco *Pacha (closed Sun–Wed | www.pacha-muenchen.de)* where your ears will buzz to the sound of Ibiza house music of course. Nextdoor, in the flirters' stronghold *089 Bar (closed Sun, Mon | www.089-bar.de)*, the permanent mixture of hits from the past 50 years gets people in the mood. On Thu and Fri, Pacha and 089 join up and charge a single entrance fee for both clubs. An absolute contrast can be found in the basement at the *Rote Sonne (closed Sun–Wed | www.rote-sonne.com)*. Electro and minimal call the tune in this underground eldorado. *Max & Moritz (closed Sun–Wed | www.maxundmoritz.tv)* is also subterranean but much more commercial and for a generally younger clientele. It stretches over two levels and is known

for its really low-priced drinks. Chic *Baby! (closed Sun–Wed | www.babymunich.com)* is at the other end of the price scale. If you manage to get through the door, you'll come face to face with football stars, young actors and models who order champagne and vodka by the bottle. The easy-listening electro music comes free of charge. Those who prefer things a bit more casual and a lot more colourful should cross the road and face the LEDs and loud music in *Chaca Chaca (closed Sun–Thu | Maximiliansplatz 16 | www.chaca-chaca.de)*. *U/S-Bahn Karlsplatz (Stachus)*

OPTIMOLWERKE (135 E5) (*W L8–9*)

On a site next to the Kultfabrik, this party complex, with some dozen locations be-

Munich nightlife: partying it away in stylish venues

hind the Ostbahnhof, is the smaller of the two. The spectrum ranges from the huge disco *Spielwiese* to the house club *Bullitt* and Latin bar *Do Brasil. Daily | Friedenstr. 10 | www.optimolwerke.de | U/S-Bahn Ostbahnhof*

P1 (134 C1) *(ω J6)*
Completely revamped in 2010, P 1 now has a superb music system, better sited DJ consoles in both sections, and carefully designed spaces even down to the loos – and they're really quite something. The INSIDER TIP ▶ Asian food is tasty too. A good alternative to the former pizza special. *Daily | Prinzregentenstr. 1 | www.p1-club. de | U4/5 Lehel*

PARADISO
(127 D5) *(ω H8)*
A bar with a dance floor and a history: this is where Freddie Mercury, David Bowie and Mick Jagger once partied the night away. Glass chandeliers, red velvet and huge mirrors make one's heart beat faster. Striking up a conversation here is not a problem. Any number of hits and classics get people in a party mood. Arrive early as the queue is sometimes very long. *Closed Sun–Wed | Rumfordstr. 2 | www. paradiso-tanzbar.de | tram 16/18 Reichenbachplatz*

PIMPERNEL (126 B6) *(ω H8)*
Even before World War II there was a nightclub of the site. Later, it turned into a gay bar where Freddy Mercury used to hang out and where, supposedly, the Munich actor Walter Sedlmayr met his murderer. Now the 'in' crowd has discovered it along with its slightly disreputable image, and parties almost every day into the early hours. *Daily | Müllerstraße 56 | www.pimpernel-muenchen.de | U1/2/3/6 Sendlinger Tor*

SONNENSTRASSE ★
(126 B4–5) *(ω H7)*
While Munich's nightlife was still centred on the Kunstpark behind the Ostbahnhof at the end of the '90s, it's now 'back to the roads' of the city centre. And it's on Sonnenstraße that the party-goer's heart beats faster. Starting at Sendlinger Tor is *8 Seasons (closed Sun, Mon, Wed, Thu | Sonnenstr. 26 | www.8-seasons.com)* –

the annual New Year's Eve gala event. *Haimhauser/Ursulastraße | tel. 39 19 97 | www.lachundschiess.de | U3/6 Münchner Freiheit*

MÜNCHNER LUSTSPIELHAUS
(131 D4) (*M K4*)

Some times singer-songwriters, other times cabarets or *concertantes*. High-quality entertainment in plush surroundings with many local cult names: the 'Isar Indian' Willy Michl, the political German/Turkish cabaretist Django Asül, or the unimatable Austrian Wolfgang Ambros. *Daily | Occamstr. 8 | tel. 34 49 74 | www. lustspielhaus.de | U3/6 Münchner Freiheit*

SCHLACHTHOF – WIRTSHAUS & BÜHNE (133 F4) (*M G9*)

In 1987, Franz Xaver Bogner brought the cult series *Zur Freiheit* into German sitting rooms and made the 'meat-packing district' famous as a result. This pub restaurant played a pivotal role during filming. The venue is used for cabarets, concerts and parties. Good hearty fare is served. *Zenettistr. 9 | tel. 72 62 56 20 | www.im-schlachthof.de | U3/6 Poccistraße*

now with rather mainstream music and clienele – housed in an imposing brick building. On the same side of the road towards Stachus the next place of note is the *Cord Club (closed Sun–Tue | Sonnenstraße 18 | www.cord-muenchen.de)* on the first floor of the corner building. Is it worth going up there? Definitely! Lots of retro to charm you, laid back mid-20-somethings and Indie pearls from the DJs. Slightly different sounds (charts, dance) are spun on the turntables a few yards further on in *Milchbar (closed Sun | Sonnenstr. 12 | www.milchundbar.de)*. Also located on the first floor, this is still a flirter's paradise. This is also true for *X-Cess (daily | Sonnenstr. 8)*. If you're not afraid of any kind of music or body contact then this weird dive run by the former doner kebab proprietor, Isi Yilmaz, is the place for you. *U1/2/3/6 Sendlinger Tor*

CABARET & FRINGE THEATRE

LACH & SCHIESSGESELLSCHAFT ★
(131 D4) (*M K4*)

Still Munich's best-known cabaret. The audience is packed in like sardines. Tip:

CINEMAS

CINEMA ★
(129 F6) (*M G6*)

Best original-language selection of films, known for its double and triple features. *Nymphenburger Str. 31 | tel. 55 52 55 | www.cinema-muenchen.com | U1 Stiglmaierplatz*

INSIDER TIP ▶ MUSEUMSLICHTSPIELE
(134 C3) (*M J–K8*)

Since 1910 film stars have flickered across the screens of this small but charming cinema. Nowadays, most are in English. The classic is *The Rocky Horror Picture Show*, that has been running here for 30 years!

Very good children's films. *Lilienstr. 2 | tel. 089 48 24 03 | http://muenchen.movie town.eu | tram 16 Deutsches Museum*

NEUES ROTTMANN (134 A1) *(⛺ G6)*
Art-house cinema with top-level repertoire. A must for film freaks. *Rottmannstr. 15 | tel. 089 52 16 83 | www.neuesrottmann. de | U1 Stiglmaierplatz*

PUBS

FRAUNHOFER SCHOPPENSTUBE (134 B3) *(⛺ H8)*
Weird dive which draws night owls from the Glockenbach district very late at night – or early in the morning. Cross the threshold and you'll be greeted by the landlady, Gerti, known throughout the city for her somewhat vulgar language and her one or other musical rendition. For the hungry, roast pork is available until the early hours. *Closed Tue | Fraunhoferstr. 41 | www. fraunhofer-schoppenstube.bei-gerti.de | U1/2 Fraunhoferstraße*

LOW BUDGET

▶ Club and Line: the Partybus with a bar and DJ runs until the early hours (Fri, Sat) between popular clubs in the city – a cheap and fun alternative to a taxi. For an up-to-date route plan and prices see: *www.club-and-line.de.*

▶ *Barschwein* is the cheapest 'in' bar in town (Pils beer for 1 euro)! And even its location plumb in the middle of Schwabing is super – not to mention the sleazy red décor. *Daily | (131 D4) (⛺ J4) | Siegesstr. 19 | www.barschwein.de | U3/6 Münchner Freiheit*

NED KELLY'S (127 D4) *(⛺ H7)*
Australians love friends, parties and beer which means that nobody is left standing on their own for long in this pub right next to the cathedral. If there's nothing to celebrate (football) then some reason will be found and Victoria beer tapped til the barrels run dry. *Daily | Frauenplatz 11 | U/S-Bahn Marienplatz*

STADION AN DER SCHLEISSHEIMER STRASSE (130 A5) *(⛺ G5)*
A stadium in the 'pub' section? No, it's not a printing mistake. This special spectator arena with beer on tap is a bastion for football fans. One huge screen, artificial grass on the ceiling, fan paraphernalia on the walls, cramped seating like in a real stadium – what more could you want? Even TV sports channels regularly report live from this pub to see what the mood is like. *Daily | Schleissheimer Str. 82 | www. stadionanderschleissheimerstraße.de | U2 Theresienstraße*

CONCERTS & OPERAS

HERKULESSAAL ⭐ (127 E2) *(⛺ J7)*
Classical music in a Classicist setting. The Hercules Hall in the Residenz is a mecca for Munich's concert-goers. *Residenzstr. 1 (entrance from the Hofgarten) | tel. 089 29 06 71 | U3/4/5/6 Odeonsplatz*

NATIONALTHEATER (127 E3) *(⛺ J7)*
Munich's opera house, the No. 1 spot with regard to both the quality of the performances and the amount it is subsidised. *Max-Joseph-Platz 2 | tel. 089 21 85 01 | www.bayerische.staatsoper.de | tram 19 Nationaltheater*

PRINZREGENTENTHEATER (133 E2) *(⛺ L7)*
Grand reconstruction of the former opera house. Today, chiefly used as a concert

hall, it prides itself on its excellent acoustics – the best in town. Wonderful café. *Prinzregentenplatz 12 | tel. 089 21 85 02 | www.prinzregententheater.de | U4 Prinzregentenplatz*

CULTURAL CENTRES

GASTEIG (135 D3) *(ω K8)*

The home of the Munich Philharmonic Orchestra is not only devoted to classical music. The Gasteig is also a magnet for jazz, exhibitions and cinema-related events, hosting the International Film Festival at the end of July. This huge complex on the east bank of the Isar also houses the municipal library where numerous readings and lectures are held, as well as the adult education centre. *Rosenheimer Str. 5 | tel. 089 48 09 80 | www.gasteig.de | S-Bahn Rosenheimer Platz*

INSIDER TIP PASINGER FABRIK (138 C3) *(ω 0)*

One of the most ambitious cultural projects in the city was launched in Pasing, of all places, where the residents still look on themselves as coming from Pasing and not Munich. In the old factory building, exhibitions, plays and concerts are held. The Theater Rote Rüben and Munich's smallest opera house are also based here. *Closed Mon | August-Exter-Str. 1 | tel. 089 82 92 90 79 | www.pasinger-fabrik.com | S-Bahn Pasing*

MUSIC PUBS & CLUBS

59:1 (126 B5) *(ω H7)*

In 59:1, the Red Hot Chili Peppers grin down at you from the wall while Indie pop and punk bands from around the globe on the stage get the audience going. The proprietor Frank Bergmeyer is often in the front row himself. *Daily | Sonnenstr. 27 | www.59to1.net | U1/2/3/6 Sendlinger Tor*

Concert hall, festival centre, municipal library: the Gasteig has many facets

ATOMIC CAFÉ ★ (127 E4) *(ω J7)*

Listen to hip bands such as Sportfreunde Stiller in the retro lounge of Munich's Brit pop and Indie rock fans. *Closed Sun, Mon | Neuturmstr. 5 | www.atomic.de | U/S-Bahn Marienplatz*

BACKSTAGE (132 C1) *(ω D6)*

Hard and heavy, loud, young and freaky. Backstage is more or less the city's crossover mecca, but reggae and electronic fans also feel at home here. Three separate music areas and a cosy beer garden open in the evenings provide a lot of variety for a mixed public. *Daily | Reitknechtstr. 6 | tel. 089 126 61 00 | www.backstage.eu | S-Bahn Hirschgarten*

JAZZCLUB UNTERFAHRT (135 E2) *(ω L7)*

For a reasonable admission charge, jazz fans can usually listen to the high-class Munich jazz scene plus big international stars. Jam sessions every Sunday evening. *Daily | Einsteinstr. 42 | www.unterfahrt.de | U4/5 Max-Weber-Platz*

The Cuvilliés Theatre – Europe's most beautiful Rococo theatre

MUFFATWERK (135 D3) (*[illustration] K8*)

This attractive Jugendstil building used to be a power plant. Today, it's Munich's culture vultures who work up a heat at concerts, dances, plays and other performances. Subsidised sub-culture, a great café, the 'in' club *Ampere (Fri, Sat)* and, in summer, a INSIDER TIP romantic beer garden with 🙂 organic meat specialities, vegetarian and Mediterranean dishes. *Daily | Zellstr. 4 | tel. 089 45 87 50 10 | www.muffathalle. de | S-Bahn Rosenheimer Platz or Isartor*

NIGHT CLUB IM BAYERISCHEN HOF (127 D3) (*[illustration] H7*)

Munich's most prestigious jazz venue with international greats from Klaus Doldinger to Joe Zawinul making guest appearances. While elsewhere in the city, the few jazz clubs still left are closing their doors, music is alive and kicking here – thanks to the subsidies from the hotel. The drinks may be expensive, but, from a musical point of view, you won't have to take much

of a risk here. *Daily | Promenadeplatz 2–6 | www.bayerischerhof.de | U/S-Bahn Karlsplatz (Stachus), tram 19 Theatinerstraße*

SUBSTANZ (133 F4) (*[illustration] F9*)

A live music institution for more than 20 years. In the early days, grunge and hardcore bands held sway, but now the sounds of Indie rock can be heard (also on the venue's own Internet radio station) as well as cult-like readings. The DJs put the boat out too while the fight is on at the football table. *Daily | Ruppertstr. 28 | www. substanz-club.de | U3/6 Poccistraße*

VOGLER (127 E5) (*[illustration] J7–8*)

Great jazz pub near Gärtnerplatz. Although the big names of old only appear here rarely, local heroes such as Joe Kienemann and Ecco di Lorenzo ensure that guests order another glass of wine or lager. The reasonable entrance fee is added to your bill at the end. *Closed Sun | Rumfordstr. 17 | www.jazzbar-vogler.com | S-Bahn Isartor*

THEATRES

CUVILLIÉS THEATER ⭐
(127 E3) (*J7*)

A masterpiece of courtly Rococo architecture – and a reconstruction, created at the insistence of the people of Munich after the original palace theatre was destroyed in World War II. The old theatre was the setting for numerous magnificent opera productions, including the premiere of Mozart's Idomeneo around 1781. Reopened after renovation in 2008, it has become the stage for successful established theatre. *Residenzstr. 1 | tel. 089 21 85 01 | www.resi denztheater.de | tram 19 Max-Joseph-Platz*

DEUTSCHES THEATER (138 C3) (*O*)

Almost everything is on offer here – from carnival balls to operettas and singer-songwriter concerts. While the building in Schwanthalerstraße is undergoing renovation, productions are being held in a luxurious circus marquee next to the Allianz Arena in Fröttmaning until 2013. *Werner-Heisenberg-Allee 11 | tel. 089 55 23 44 44 | www.deutsches-theater.de | U6 Fröttmaning*

GOP VARIETÉTHEATER (134 C2) (*J7*)

Every two months the music hall programme with acrobats and comedians changes, put together by the variety show specialists at GOP who operate throughout Germany. Guests can choose between enjoying the show on its own or having a set-course meal in the evening to accompany an opulent dinner spectacle. *Maximilianstr. 47 | tel. 089 2 10 28 84 44 | www.variete.de/muenchen | tram 17/19 Maxmonument*

MÜNCHNER KAMMERSPIELE (SCHAUSPIELHAUS) (127 F4) (*J7*)

The Jugendstil building on Maximilianstraße has been home to the country's leading theatre since 1926 which the many awards go to prove. In 2009, the Kammerspiele was nominated 'Theatre of the Year'. The Dutch director, Johan Simons, for whom Munich is just perfect for creating something between art and reality, greatly values works by Michel Houellebecq, Elfriede Jelinek, Lion Feuchtwanger, Ödön von Horváth, Heinrich von Kleist, Luchino Visconti, Luis Buñuel and Stanley Kubrick. *Maximilianstraße 28 | tel. 089 23 39 66 00 | www. muenchner-kammerspiele.de | U3/4/5/6 Odeonsplatz*

RESIDENZTHEATER
(127 E3) (*J7*)

After the successful director Dieter Dorn's term was over, the Austrian, Martin Kušej, took up his new position in 2011 and immediately set about making radical changes to the ensemble and choice of plays. His mini cultural revolution is aimed at drawing greater international attention to the theatre. This also goes for the orgy of premieres – 27 alone in the first theatre season. The public can look forward to stars such as Tobias Moretti and Birgit Minichmayr who are now permanent members of the ensemble. *Max-Joseph-Platz 1 | tel. 089 21 85 01 | www.residenz theater.de | U3/4/5/6 Odeonsplatz*

VOLKSTHEATER
(134 A1) (*G6*)

In autumn 2002, Christian Stückl – who has directed the Passion Play in Oberammergau and staged 'Jedermann' in Salzburg – took over the management of this theatre – one of the city's major financial headaches. Classics including 'The Threepenny Opera' and radically modern theatre ensure that performances are regularly booked out. *Brienner Str. 50 | tel. 089 5 23 46 55 | www.muenchner-volkstheater.de | U1 Stiglmaierplatz*

WHERE TO STAY

Fans of the German TV series 'Kir Royal' know the luxurious surroundings in which well-heeled visitors to the city spend the night – be it in the king's or prince's suites, which can well set you back 2000 euros a night. But, if you're not careful, even your average visitor to Munich can end up paying a fortune. That's particularly true during the Oktoberfest or when major trade fairs are on, when prices can double.

However, apart from the famous palatial hotels, the city has a whole range of medium-sized to small hotels and guesthouses which, on average, are only half full throughout the year. Hotels often have special rates – but only if you ask. Comparing prices when you arrive is also worthwhile. Check if the hotel is conveniently located for the public transport system as driving and parking in the city centre is strenuous for everyone and not just visitors. Many hotels can be found under *www.deutschland-hotel.de,* on the tourist office website *www.muenchen.de/int/en* or under *www.nethotels.com.*

HOTELS: EXPENSIVE

ANNA HOTEL ★ (126 A3) *(ᴍ G7)*
With busy Stachus in front and the main station behind, getting here couldn't be

A good night's sleep: from luxury hotels to youth hostels – Munich has accommodation to suit every budget

easier. And thanks to soundproofed windows you'll have a peaceful night's sleep. The good-feel factor is heightened by the spacious, modern rooms. The highlights: the Panorama Room and the Tower Suite, both with private balconies and wonderful views. From the latter, you even have a view over Munich from the bathtub. The *Anna Restaurant (Moderate)*, serving not only first-rate sushi but also other delicacies, belongs to the hotel. *73 rooms | Schützenstr. 1 | tel. 089 59 99 40 | www.annahotel.de | U/S-Bahn Karlsplatz (Stachus)*

CORTIINA ☺
(127 E4) (ᗞ J7)
In Munich, the names Kull & Weinzierl stand for quality gastronomy and design. This is also reflected in their first hotel that

they opened in 2001 right in the heart of the city. The specially designed furniture is only made of solid wood, the cotton bed linen is hand sewn and the floors are

Hotel Cocoon: colourful, cheerful, stylish and functional

of oak parquet with natural Jurassic stone in the bathrooms. The hotel bar has developed into a popular meeting place where first-class cocktails are served. *35 rooms | Ledererstr. 8 | tel. 089 2 42 24 90 | www.cortiina.com | U/S-Bahn Marienplatz*

FLEMING'S

Both the hotel in Schwabing and its 4-star twin near the station stand out due to their modern flair. Large glazed walls let light flood into the lobby and restaurant *(Moderate)*, which serves grilled and sea-food dishes as well as French brasserie specialities. Dark wood has been used in the rooms. INSIDER TIP Direct booking possible using Fleming's app. *www.flemings-hotels.com; 122 rooms | (133 F2) (Ø G7) | Bayerstr. 47 | tel. 089 4 44 46 60 | U/S-Bahn Hauptbahnhof; 168 rooms | (130 C3) (Ø J3) | Leopoldstr. 130–132 | tel. 089 206 09 00 | U6 Dietlindenstraße*

H'OTELLO ADVOKAT B'01
(127 F5) (Ø J8)

This designer hotel is one of the best of its kind in Munich. The combination of art, interior design, lighting and service creates an atmosphere that never gives you the feeling you're just passing through. On top of this, the location couldn't be better, just a few minutes walk from Marienplatz and the Deutsches Museum. *50 rooms | Baaderstraße 1 | tel. 089 21 63 10 | www.hotel-advokat.de | S-Bahn Isartor*

INSIDER TIP HOTEL LUX
(127 E4) (Ø J7)

The Lux has a charm of its own that is reflected in the retro look colours of the rooms decorated in the 70s-style. One eye-opener is the 'Birdroom', designed by 'Birdman' – the artist Hans Langner. The staircase is listed. The lovingly designed restaurant *(Expensive)* spoils guests in its plush surroundings with cooking of an extremely high quality. *17 rooms | Lederer-straße 13 | tel. 089 45 20 73 00 | www.hotel-lux.info | U/S-Bahn Marienplatz*

PALACE (135 E2) (Ø L7)

Small, personal, luxury hotel much valued by stars such as Robbie Williams and Anna Netrebko. This is enhanced by the lovely, peaceful garden and the unusual furnishings including Louis XVI-style works of art. Art and culture weekend rates. *81 rooms | Trogerstr. 21 | tel. 089 41 97 10 |*

www.kuffler.de/palace | U4 Prinzregentenplatz

RITZI (135 D2) (*M K7*)

No two rooms are the same here as each has its own theme. In the Chinese Room, the walls are decorated with calligraphy and large carved wood pictures; the furniture is also from China. For those struck by Cupid's arrow, the Red Room or White Room is best for a romantic night, depending on how you feel. Anyone with a longing for the sea should plump for the stylish maritime cabin. The Ritzi also has a classical bar and restaurant *(Expensive)* that is equally popular among locals. *25 rooms | Maria-Theresia-Str. 2 a | tel. 089 4 14 24 08 90 | www.hotel-ritzi.de | U4/5 Max-Weber-Platz*

HOTELS: MODERATE

ART HOTEL MUNICH
(133 F2) (*M G7*)

The rooms with their dark parquet floors, light coloured walls, comfortable sofas and large beds are modern and cosy. Temporary exhibitions of works by young artists are part of the hotel's contemporary approach as is the cooperation with the hip *Body-&-Soul Fitnessstudio* (day pass 15 euros). *110 rooms | Paul-Heyse-Str. 10 | tel. 089 30 90 66 30 | www.arthotel munich.com | U/S-Bahn Hauptbahnhof*

INSIDER TIP ▶ BLAUER BOCK
(127 D5) (*M H7*)

This traditional hotel near the Viktualienmarkt that has existed since 1572 has undergone a very successful makeover. But what makes it an absolute hotspot is the price. That you can only pay with an EC or Amex card, or in cash, is really not a big problem. What you save can be spent in the adjoining restaurant *(Moderate–Expensive)* run by the Witzigmann-pupil

Hans Jörg Bachmeier. *69 rooms | Sebastiansplatz 9 | tel. 089 23 17 80 | www.hotelblauerbock.de | U/S-Bahn Marienplatz*

COCOON ★ (126 A6) (*M G8*)

Colourful designer gem with a flashy '70s look. This stylish hotel has not only been given awards for its chic, functional rooms and the service, but also for is very civil pricing policy. A great advantage is that the eternally hip Glockenbach district and the new nightlife drag on Sonnenstraße are just a hop, skip and jump away. *46*

MARCO POLO HIGHLIGHTS

★ **Anna Hotel**
Urban surroundings, modern design and wonderful views
→ p. 93

★ **Cocoon**
Colourful 'flower power' design close to the clubbing district
→ p. 95

★ **Bayerischer Hof**
Luxury hotel, much loved by the people of Munich too
→ p. 96

★ **Louis**
High ecological standards in one of the best designed hotels in Europe
→ p. 96

★ **Mariandl**
Like a journey back in time to the turn of the 20th century
→ p. 99

★ **Motel One**
A new hotel generation with regard to price and design
→ p. 100

rooms | Lindwurmstr. 35 | tel. 089 59 99 39 07 | www.hotel-cocoon.de | U1/2/3/6 Sendlinger Tor

HOTEL ENGLISCHER GARTEN
(131 D4) *(ᗄ K4)*

This listed villa is set against the backdrop of the English Garden. Just a short walk to the west and you'll find yourself in the heart of legendary Schwabing where you can go on a shopping spree or immerse yourself in the nightlife. *26 rooms | Liebergesellstr. 8 | tel. 089 3 83 94 10 | www.hotelenglischergarten.de | U3/6 Münchner Freiheit*

HOTEL HERZOG
(133 F4) *(ᗄ G8)*

Mediterranean-styled rooms around a courtyard that, with its Tuscan look com-

LUXURY HOTELS

Bayerischer Hof ⭐ (127 D3) *(ᗄ H7)*

Aristocrats and the moneyed favour this Classicist building right in the city centre. Nonetheless, special offers are often available. Double rooms from 420 euros, suites from 1800 euros. *350 rooms | Promenadeplatz 2 | tel. 089 2 12 00 | www.bayerischerhof.de | U/S-Bahn Karlsplatz (Stachus)*

The Charles Hotel (126 A2) *(ᗄ G6)*

Enjoy the view of the Old Botanical Garden and an 8600ft² spa complex. Double rooms from 295 euros, suites from 435 euros. *160 rooms | Sophienstraße 28 | tel. 089 5 44 55 50 | www.charleshotel.de | U/S-Bahn Karlsplatz (Stachus)*

Kempinski Hotel Vier Jahreszeiten (127 F3) *(ᗄ J7)*

Built by Elector Maximilian II, the hotel is located on Munich's most expensive shopping street. The elegant restaurant *Vue Maximilian (Expensive)* can be highly recommended. Double rooms from 255 euros, suites from 650 euros. *303 rooms | Maximilianstr. 17 | tel. 089 21 25 27 99 | www.kempinski-vierjahreszeiten.de | U/S-Bahn Marienplatz*

Louis ⭐ 😊 (127 D5) *(ᗄ J7)*

Shortly after opening in 2009, it was declared Europe's best hotel by a top designer magazine. Fitted with individually made furniture to the most stringent ecological standards and with views over the Viktualienmarkt. Spa; Japanese gourmet restaurant *(Expensive)*. Double rooms from 195 euros. *72 rooms | Viktualienmarkt 6 | tel. 089 41 11 90 80 | www.louis-hotel.com | U/S-Bahn Marienplatz*

Mandarin Oriental (127 E4) *(ᗄ J7)*

In the former Antikhaus; excellent cuisine and roof-top pool. Double rooms from 405 euros, suites from 850 euros. *73 rooms | Neuturmstr. 1 | tel. 089 29 09 80 | www.mandarinoriental.com | U/S-Bahn Marienplatz*

Sofitel Bayerpost (133 F2) *(ᗄ G7)*

Luxury hotel at the southen entrance to the main railway station with a Presidential Suite extending over 1900ft², an elegant bar and exclusive service. Double rooms from 169 euros, suites from 260 euros. *396 rooms | Bayerstr. 12 | tel. 089 59 94 80 | www.sofitel.com | U/S-Bahn Hauptbahnhof*

plete with a fountain and olive tree, is just perfect for an intimate summer evening. The gourmet breakfast buffet is worth a special mention. A glance at the hotel's website is a good idea as special offers are always clearly advertised. *80 rooms | Häberlstr. 9 | tel. 089 59 99 39 01 | www. hotel-herzog.de | U3/6 Goetheplatz*

H'OTELLO

Whether in Fallmerayerstraße or Hohenzollernstraße, both of these H'Otellos are in Schwabing and furnished in a minimalistic and timeless style. The 'Weekend Plus' package (2 nights for 2 in a double room with breakfast buffet and a day pass partner ticket for local transport) is available from 149 euros. *73 rooms | (130 B4) (Ⓜ H4) | Fallmerayerstr. 22 | tel. 089 3 07 92 00 | U2 Hohenzollernplatz; 71 rooms | (130 C5) (Ⓜ J4) | Hohenzollernstr. 9 | tel. 089 309 07 70 | U3/6 Giselastraße | www.hotello.de*

HOTEL KRIEMHILD
(126 B6) *(Ⓜ C5)*

Small, friendly, private guesthouse which also has 4-bed rooms. Both Nymphenburg Palace as well as the Museum Natur und Mensch are just a few minutes walk away. And Munich's biggest beer garden, the Hirschgarten, is more or less right on the doorstep. If you stay longer than 7 nights, you get 1 night free. *18 rooms | Guntherstr. 16 | tel. 089 17 11 11 70 | www.kriemhild.de | tram 16/17 Kriemhildenstraße*

LEOPOLD
(130 C3) *(Ⓜ J3)*

In the Roaring Twenties this was the first and only hotel in Schwabing. The Leopold, that has been in the same family for five generations, not only has a peaceful location, a large garden and excellent public transport connections, but stands out in particular for its friendly service – some-

thing many regular guests can confirm. *100 rooms | Leopoldstr. 119 | tel. 089 36 70 61 | www.hotel-leopold.de | U6 Dietlindenstraße*

PENSION GÄRTNERPLATZ
(127 D6) *(Ⓜ H8)*

Surrounded by galleries, boutiques, cafés, bars and restaurants, this little guest-

Mediterranean flair in the courtyard at the Hotel Herzog

house has an atmosphere that is only rarely found in Munich. Each of the 10 rooms is furnished with great attention to detail and to a particular motto – which means that even King Ludwig II watches over sleeping guests. *10 rooms | Klenzestr. 45 | tel. 089 202 51 70 | www.pension gaertnerplatz.de | U1/2 Fraunhoferstraße*

HOTELS: BUDGET

GOLDEN LEAF HOTEL ALTMÜNCHEN
(134 C4) (Ø J8)

The small 'old Bavarian' hotel is right on Mariahilfplatz. The beds have fluffy soft duvets. Just a few minutes walk to the Deutsches Museum, the Nockherberg, the Müllersches Volksbad and the Gasteig cultural centre. *32 rooms | Mariahilfplatz*

Only 3 underground stops to the Allianz Arena. *132 rooms | Frankfurter Ring 243 | tel. 089 3 06 58 90 | www.hotelbb.de | U6 Studentenstadt*

CREATIF HOTEL ELEPHANT ☺
(133 F2) (Ø G6)

'Green' 3-star hotel as the wood used in the rooms and the oak floorboards were sourced exclusively in Europe. Buffet break-

Plain but cosily colourful: the façade of the Creatif Hotel Elephant

4 | tel. 089 45 84 40 | www.golden-leaf-hotel.de | Bus 52/152 Schweigerstraße

INSIDER TIP ▶ B & B HOTELS
(131 E1) (Ø L1)

This budget chain has three hotels in and around Munich, but only the one on Frankfurter Ring is actually in the city. A simple, colourful design and functional style is coupled with an extremely moderate pricing policy. 2 adults and 2 children, for example, can stay here from 79 euros.

fast included in the price. The Augustiner beer garden is just 5 mins. away. *45 rooms | Lämmerstr. 6 | tel. 089 55 57 85 | www. creatif-hotel-elephant.com | U/S-Bahn Hauptbahnhof*

HOTEL DOLOMIT
(133 F2) (Ø G7)

Thanks to its central location just a few yards from the main station, those arriving by air and rail never need to take a taxi. This 2-star B&B has five floors with rooms of varying categories from the simple to more comfortable. **INSIDER TIP** 10% discount for advance bookings. *91 rooms | Goethestraße 11 | tel. 089 59 28 47 | www.hotel-dolomit.de | U/S-Bahn Hauptbahnhof*

EASY PALACE STATION HOTEL
(126 A3) (*∅ G7*)

Low-priced red-and-white Ikea look, some rooms with basic sanitary facilities. 4 categories of room from the basic (washbasin in room, shared WC on landing, no shower) to the deluxe (en suite bathroom, TV and breakfast incl.). 4–6 bed dormitory-style rooms, suitable for groups or families, have shower/WC on the landing. Can't get much more central than this. *55 rooms | Schützenstr. 7 | tel. 089 5 52 52 10 | www. easypalace.de | U/S-Bahn Hauptbahnhof*

G HOTEL
(134 B4) (*∅ H8*)

This former post-office apartment building is just a stone's throw from the Isar. The Deutsches Museum, the Glockenbach and Gärtnerplatz districts as well as the Viktualienmarkt can all be reached on foot. The rooms are spacious and bright. Tip for film fans: the 'Bavaria Filmstadt' package includes B&B for 1 night, an MVV public transport pass, plus tickets for a tour of the Bavaria Filmstudio. *154 rooms | Baaderstr. 88–90 | tel. 089 12 71 80 | www.ghotel. de | U1/2 Fraunhoferstraße*

HOTEL AM SENDLINGER TOR
(126 C5) (*∅ H7*)

Light-coloured parquet floors and pine are features of this 2-star hotel. The rooms are clean but very simply furnished. For the thrifty: free mineral water and, if you stay for more than 7 nights, 1 night is free. *50 rooms | Oberanger 47 | tel. 089 23 07 69 73 | www.cityhotel-munich.de | U1/2/3/6 Sendlinger Tor*

MARIANDL ★
(133 F3) (*∅ G8*)

Staying here is something special. Both outside and in, this hotel – built in 1899 – is a real gem. All rooms are individual and tastefully furnished with antiques. And, as was often the case around 1900, there are still rooms with showers and WCs on the landing – not necessarily to everyone's taste. A hearty breakfast can be enjoyed in the café on the ground floor that is not only the oldest 'concert café' in town but also has excellent live music. Thanks to its proximity to the Theresienwiese, even Oktoberfest visitors can find their own way home. *28 rooms | Goethestr. 51 | tel. 089 5 52 91 00 | www.mariandl. com | U3/6 Goetheplatz*

LOW BUDGET

▶ Private rooms and apartments are often a low-priced alternative to a hotel. The agencies *Statthotel* (www.statthotel.de/home.html), *Check-In* (www.checkin-muenchen. de/index.php?), *www.bedandbutter. de/en, www.bed-and-breakfast.de/ regional_e/munich.html, www.mr lodge.de/en* and *gloveler.com* have rooms available from 30 euros a day.

▶ *The Tent:* Accommodation for backpackers and nature-lovers. Open mid June–Oct, guests sleep in one huge tent (10.50 euros for a bunk bed or 7.50 euros on a mat). Free sightseeing trips of the city available. **(128 A3)** (*∅ B3*) | *In den Kirschen 30 | tel. 089 141 43 00 | www.the-tent.com | tram 17 Botanischer Garten*

YOUTH ACCOMMODATION & HOSTELS

MEININGER HOTEL CITY CENTER
(133 E2) (*ØJ F7*)

A hint of malt lingers in the air in this district as the Augustiner brewery and pub are on the other side of the road. You can choose between 2-star single, double and multiple occupancy rooms as well as 2 dormitories sleeping 6 and 14. *95 rooms | Landsberger Straße 20 | tel. 089 54 99 80 23 | www.meininger-hotels.com | S-Bahn Hackerbrücke*

MOTEL ONE ★

The hotel chain now has 6 top designer hotels in Munich that are always pretty full. Book well in advance! The buffet breakfast is not included in the price. Families are welcome: children under 12 can stay free of charge in their parents' room. The under-6s get a free breakfast too. *www.motel-one.de, 241 rooms | (135 E3) (ØJ H7) | Herzog-Wilhelm-Str. 28 | tel. 089 51 77 72 50 | U1/2/3/6 Sendlinger Tor, 442 rooms | (135 D4) (ØJ K8) | Rabl-straße 2 | tel. 089 44 45 55 80 | S-Bahn Rosenheimer Platz, 121 rooms | (133 D2) (ØJ E7) | Landsberger Str. 79 | tel. 089 53 88 68 90 | S-Bahn Donnersberger Brücke, 219 rooms | (135 E3) (ØJ L8) | Orleanstraße 87 | tel. 089 59 97 64 90 | U/S-Bahn Ostbahnhof, 252 rooms | (138 C3) (ØJ J11) | Weissenseestr. 140 | tel. 089 69 80 42 10 | U1 Wettersteinplatz*

YOUTH ACCOMMODATION & HOSTELS

A&O HOSTEL ☼
(135 E1) (*ØJ F6*)

Munich's largest hostel and hotel complex with more than 1000 beds. Those who prefer a bit more comfort than a sleeping bag can choose a 2-star room in the hotel section. The large roof terrace and the hostel's own laundrette are plus points. *300 rooms | Arnulfstr. 102 | tel. 089 45 23 59 58 01 | www.aohostels.com | S-Bahn Hackerbrücke*

KEEP FIT

Running, skating, climbing – Munich is a sporty city where people jog in all seasons. The favourite routes are through the English Garden and along the Isar. If you prefer to be with others, just turn up to a free *HVB-BKK run* led by a sports instructor *(Tue, Thu 7pm | meeting point HVB-Club | (131 E5) (ØJ K8) | Am Eisbach 5 | www.hvb-bkk. de/Laufen)*.

Apart from cyclists, inline skaters speed along the tarmaced paths by the river and the 1200km (750mi)-long cycle path network. On Mondays, you can cruise through the city with thousands of locals at Europe's largest ● skating event *(May–Sept Mon 8pm | meeting point: Alte Kongresshalle, Bavariapark | (133 E2) (ØJ F8) | Theresienhöhe 15 | www.muenchner-bladenight.de)*. Traffic is diverted away from the route. Equipment available free of charge. The world's largest climbing complex is also in Munich and demands a lot of muscle power and body control. Climbing routes are available both in and outside the *DAV-Kletterzentrum (Mon–Fri 7am–11pm, Sat, Sun 8am–11pm | entrance fee 15.50 euros | (136 C1–2) (ØJ F11) | Thalkirchner Str. 207 | www.kletterzentrum-muenchen.de)*.

Good design is not necessarily a question of the price: Motel One

DJH BURG SCHWANECK
(0) (*M 0*)

Don't be put off by the label 'youth hostel' – the days of frugal living are long over. This historical building complete with a great hall, dates from 1843 and offers good hostel standard accommodation. Breakfast included in the price. 2–12 bed rooms available. *138 beds | closed mid Dec–early Jan | Burgweg 4–6 | tel. 089 74 48 66 70 | www.pullach.jugendherberge. de | S-Bahn Pullach*

DJH MUNICH PARK (136 C3) (*M F12*)
Surrounded by greenery and just a few minutes walk from the Isar, this completely renovated hostel is in tip-top condition. 2, 3, 4 and 6 bed rooms are available (from 69 euros). A hearty buffet breakfast is included in the price. *366 beds | Miesingstr. 4 | tel. 089 78 57 67 70 | www.muenchen-park.jugendherberge. de | U3 Thalkirchen*

EASY PALACE CITY HOSTEL
(133 F3) (*M G8*)

Simple, practical and cheap. The bunk beds in some of the rooms may well bring back childhood memories. Underground parking and bikes for hire are available at an additional charge. *134 rooms | Mozartstr. 4 | tel. 089 5 58 79 70 | www.easypalace. de | U3/6 Goetheplatz*

4 YOU ☺ (133 F2) (*M G9*)
Hotel and hostel near the station operated by a charitable organisation and run along ecologically-friendly lines. The hotel is on the top two floors. The all-you-can-eat breakfast, included in the price, is very much a plus point. **INSIDER TIP** Pizza, pasta & co. from 2.90 euros are available in the hostel's own restaurant. If you book online, you can get a discount of up to 30%. *60 rooms | Hirtenstr. 18 | tel. 089 5 52 16 60 | www.the4you.de | U/S-Bahn Hauptbahnhof*

WALKING TOURS

The tours are marked in green in the street atlas, the pull-out map and on the back cover

1 A BRISK STROLL THROUGH CENTRAL MUNICH

Even Munich started out quite small. This can be proven on a 2.7km (1½mi) tour that you can complete in just 40 minutes around the city centre, taking in the most important sites. If you want to discover and get to know more, then plan 2–5 hours instead.

Start at the tower of the Altes Rathaus → p. 28 which now houses the Toy Museum. A few yards away is the golden Mariensäule → p. 34 in the middle of Marienplatz. The four putti represent troubles that befell the city. The lion sym-

bolises war, the basilisk the plague, the dragon hunger and the snake faithlessness. When the clock strikes 11am or noon, all heads turn to the glockenspiel on the Neues Rathaus → p. 36 and cameras are held high. Carry on to the west to where Kaufinger Tor stood until 1807. The outline of the gateway and the walls of the house where the former merchant family, the Kaufingers, once lived, can be traced in the paving outside the clothing store Hirmer. The sculpture on the corner of Kaufingerstraße/Augustinerstraße is also a reminder of the old city gate. Opposite, the basilica of the former Augustinian church now houses the Jagd und Fischerei-

Discover Munich: interesting tours around the city for those in a hurry, culture vultures, sports fans, architecture freaks and families

museum (Hunting and Fishing Museum) *(Mon–Wed, Fri–Sun 9.30am–5pm, Thu 9.30am–9pm | entrance fee 3.50 euros | www.jagd-fischerei-museum.de)*. At this point you are already beyond the boundary of 12th-century Munich.

Just round the corner is the **Frauenkirche** → p. 31, where Josef Ratzinger – now Pope Benedict XVI – was bishop and cardinal from 1977–81. The brick building has many

tales to tell, like the one of the faces that peer out from the top of the columns. These are portraits of the craftsmen who built the cathedral.

Time for your first break – e.g. in the **Hofbräuhaus** → p. 70. Take a quick look in the main hall before you go into the lovely beer garden. If it's raining, the Bräustüberl on the first floor can be recommended. Having regained your strength, continue to Isartor → p. 41, that forms part of the second city wall (1285). Climb the steps to the Valentin-Karlstadt-Musäum → p. 42 where strange things await you such as a winter toothpick. 400 exhibits later it's off to the Viktualienmarkt → p. 79 where Munich's heart beats. Just sit on a bench and watch the comings and goings or sample one or other delicacy at one of the stands. A refreshing draught beer can be had in the beer garden. A unique feature here is that – on a six-weekly rota – beer from the six different breweries in Munich is served alternately. Now move on to Alter Peter → p. 37 above the market. Legend has it that Munich was built around this, the oldest church in the city. Further left you come to Rindermarkt, the cattle market of old. Nowadays, passers-by dangle their feet in the fountain. Follow Rosenstraße back to the Neues Rathaus – a Gothic Revival building that was not completed until 1909. The tower in the Town Hall offers a wonderful view and you can see where you have just been

from high up. To gain a more in-depth impression of the city, a visit to the Stadtmuseum → p. 35 can be recommended. The permanent exhibition ● 'Typisch München' provides a good overview of the city's history.

2 A VISIT TO THE 'KUNSTAREAL' CULTURAL DISTRICT

Vienna has its Museums-Quartier, Berlin its Museumsinsel – and Munich its 'Kunstareal': a cultural district whose highlights are within walking (or cycling) distance of one another.

Those who prefer things a bit more leisurely can take the Museumslinie 100 bus that runs every 10 mins. and, in just 15 mins., travels from the main station across the Classicist Königsplatz, past the Technische Universität and the three Pinakothek museums, to Odeonsplatz and on to the Haus der Kunst. If you have

The old arsenal is now home to the Stadtmuseum

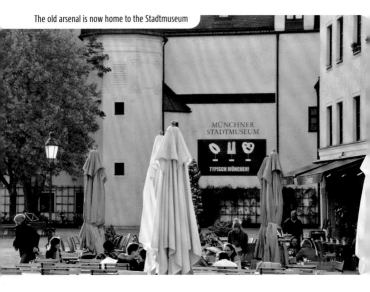

a day pass, you can break your journey as often as you like at the museum of your choice.

Your first stop should be Königsplatz → p. 46. Here you can easily see why the Munich of King Ludwig I was nicknamed 'Athens on the Isar'. Sculptures from Antiquity are on display in the Glyptothek → p. 46 whereas the Antikensammlung (Collection of Antiquities) itself focuses more on exquisite artefacts. The Lenbachhaus nearby → p. 46, the home of the Blue Rider Collection, is closed until the end of 2013 for building work. From Königsplatz, carry on to the Pinakothek museums. En route you pass the new Staatliches Museum Ägyptischer Kunst → p. 49 on the corner of Gabelsbergerstraße and Barerstraße (projected opening early 2013). Opposite is the Alte Pinakothek → p. 43 with its extensive collection of Old Masters. The lawns in front are home to one or other volleyball match in the summer – an ideal spot for a break and a bit of spectator sport. If neither Old Masters nor sport are up your street, cross over the road and head for the Pinakothek der Moderne → p. 49. This imposing building is home to modern art and design. The Museum Brandhorst → p. 48, with its brightly coloured façade, cannot be missed. The carefully planned exhibition rooms with works by Warhol, Twombly, Hirst and Co. are a feast for the eyes. If you then follow Theresienstraße a little, heading in a westerly direction, you will come to the Neue Pinakothek → p. 49, with its extensive collection of European art from the 19th century, from the Classicist to Jugendstil periods.

If, after all you have seen, you still have capacity for more, take bus no. 100 again. From the bus stop 'Pinakotheken' it is an 8-min. ride to the stop 'Nationalmuseum/ Haus der Kunst'. By bike or on foot (approx. 15 min.), head east along Gabelsberger-

straße – Oskar-von-Miller-Ring – Von-der-Tann-Straße – Prinzregentenstraße. The long colonnaded building on the left is the Haus der Kunst → p. 39 that stages temporary exhibitions of works by well-known, generally modern artists. Our cultural tour of Munich ends some 200m further down the same road at the Bayerisches Nationalmuseum → p. 39, that provides an insight into the culture and art history of Bavaria as well as regional craftsmanship. Now you can reward yourself with a relaxing stroll through the English Garden → p. 44 just round the corner.

3 MODERN ARCHITECTURE ON WHEELS

Munich is more than the cathedral, the Town Hall and the Maximilianeum. The last 30 years have seen a number of pioneering architectural projects, scattered throughout the whole city – which is why this tour is best on wheels: by bike or on inline skates. Duration: depending on how fit your are, at least 4 hours.

Take the U3 underground line to our starting point, the Olympiagelände → p. 58. The Olympic Stadium was built by one of Germany's leading architects, Günter Behnisch, for the 1972 Summer Games. There is no similar tented roof structure anywhere in the world. The stadium has become what few stadiums ever are – a symbol for the city.

Leave the Olympic Park to the east near the ice-skating rink and glide over the bridge crossing the ring road. In front of you is the world's biggest four-leaf clover: the BMW office tower → p. 57, also built in 1972 to look like a four-cylinder engine. On the other side of the road is the futuristic BMW-Welt → p. 57, a truly remarkable vehicle distribution and adventure centre.

You now come to a longer, but very attractive stretch. The North Cemetery is reached through Petuelpark and along Schenkendorfstraße. The English Garden → p. 44 starts here, which you skirt along Osterwaldstraße. Cross the ring road again and take a well-earned rest in Osterwaldgarten *(daily | Keferstr. 12 | tel. 089 38 40 50 40 | Moderate)*, before going down Kieferstraße and Mandlstraße in the prettiest part of Schwabing, to Tivolistraße, to cross the English Garden to Tucherpark. Here you'll find what was classed in the 1970s as an architectural sensation: the Bayerische Rückversicherung. The cylindrical office buildings are separated from the central services area and look as if they were built from the top downwards.

The paths of skater and cyclist part here, due to the hill to be negotiated. While skaters can treat themselves to a beer at the Chinesischer Turm → p. 62, cyclists pedal along Montgelasstraße to Effnerplatz, with its 'Mae West' sculpture by the American artist Rita McBride, that looks like a wastepaper basket! Your next stop is the Hypo-Hochhaus. Designed at the end of the '80s as a grand affirmation of capitalism, the building was once rather boldly described as 'Munich's only skyscraper' – at just 114m (374ft) – and has long been superseded. While cyclists follow Bülowstraße and Ismaninger Straße to Prinzregentenstraße, skaters – having regained their strength in the beer garden – can trundle down the pavement on Emil-Riedl-Straße towards Prinzregenten-

The architecture of the BMW-Welt is an experience itself

straße. Now orientate yourselves on the city centre to the west and head for Türkenstraße 30 (along Von-der-Tann-Straße and Theresienstraße). This is the home of the Architekturgalerie München where fascinating exhibitions on contemporary architecture and urban planning are held *(Mon–Wed 9.30am–7pm, Thu, Fri 9.30am–7.30pm, Sat 9.30am–6pm | www.architekturgalerie-muenchen.de)*. Skaters of course should have a pair of shoes in their rucksacks otherwise you won't be allowed inside!

4 TOURS FOR PARENTS AND CHILDREN

You should plan a whole day for this family outing. The actual walking time is just under an hour and the distance covered just over 4km (2½mi). Parents with toddlers should of course take a pram.

Start off in the centre, on Marienplatz → p. 34, easily reached on the underground or suburban lines. The 11m (36ft)-high Mariensäule (St Mary's Column) can't be missed. This is Munich's central point, as all streets and distances in the city are measured from here. The little uns can have a quick paddle in the Fischbrunnen → p. 34 just a few yards away where, in the olden days, fishermen used to sell the fish they had caught in the Isar. Today, it is a meeting point for locals. Now things get a little bit more strenuous – up 306 steps in the church tower in the Alter Peter → p. 37 from where you have a breath-taking view.

At lunchtime, head across the Viktualienmarkt → p. 79 into the Glockenbach district where you will reach the child-friendly, modern deli-cum-café Kaiser Otto *(daily | Westermühlstr. 8 | tel. 089 21 01 96 97 | www.kaiserotto.de)* in less than 20 mins. On some days they even

have a child-minder (tel. beforehand). From here it's not far to the most popular children's playground in the area. Walk towards Holzstraße and, after some 7 mins. (450m) you come to the Glockenbach playground complete with climbing frame, slide, swings and seesaw. Healthy refreshments are available just opposite in ☺ Naturkostladen Schmatz *(Holzstr. 49)*. Alternatively, if your children are over 4, you could pay a visit to the Münchner Marionettentheater (Puppet Theatre) → p. 108 which you pass on the way. Performances normally start at around 3pm.

From the recreation ground it's just a hop, skip and jump down Baldestraße to the Isar with its pebbly beaches which are a wonderful place for children to play. Take a gentle stoll downriver (1.7km/1mi, 30 mins.) to the Deutsches Museum → p. 51, for which you will need to plan at least one day. A detour for an hour or so to the Kinderreich (Kids' Kingdom) → p. 108, however, is a perfect way to conclude your tour and gives parents a breather too.

Children can clamber around a fire engine in 'Kids' Kingdom'

TRAVEL WITH KIDS

DEUTSCHES MUSEUM
(134 C3) (*J8*)

The museum of technology and science has its own section for budding young scientists – 'Kids' Kingdom'. Children can explore natural phenomena and even go up in the air, sit behind the steering wheel of a bright red fire engine or pluck the strings of a huge guitar. In many other departments in the museum there are lots of buttons, levers and switches to try too.

Those who would like to find out more can take a free guided tour every Wed in term time, when the world is explained to children between 4–8 years *(2.30pm–3.30pm, no reservation necessary). Daily 9am–5pm | entrance fee 8.50 euros, children 3 euros | Museumsinsel 1 | www.deutsches-museum.de | S-Bahn Isartor, tram 16 Deutsches Museum*

KINDER UND JUGENDMUSEUM
(133 F2) (*G6–7*)

The children's museum is one of the few museums where you can touch everything. Thematic exhibitions explain what is going on in and on the earth in real and digital form. *Tue–Fri 2pm–5.30pm, Sat, Sun 11am–5.30pm | entrance fee 4.50 euros, families: 2 adults, 2 children 11.50 euros | Arnulfstraße 3 | www.kindermuseum-muenchen.de | U/S-Bahn Hauptbahnhof*

MÜNCHNER MARIONETTENTHEATER
(126 C6) (*H8*)

The more than 110-year-old Puppet Theatre, with performances (in German) for children over 4 years old, is near the central fire station (another attraction especially when the doors are open). The building itself is listed. *Entrance fee 10 euros, children 8 euros | Blumenstr. 32 | www.muenchner-marionettentheater.de | U 1/2/3/6 Sendlinger Tor*

SCHAUBURG
(130 B5) (*H5*)

Young, creative theatre where bands perform, plays are staged (in German) and rock music events held. Not just for children. *Entrance fee 7 euros, children 5 euros, families: 2 adults, 1 child 15 euros, 2 adults, 2 children 25 euros | Franz-Joseph-Straße 47 | www.schauburg.net | tram 27 Elisabethplatz*

Whether budding scientists, animal lovers or theatre fans – there are many exciting things for younger visitors to do

SEA LIFE
(129 F3) (∅ G2)

Walk through the underwater tunnel and marvel at more than 10,000 fish, crabs and mussels from up close. INSIDERTIP Buy your ticket online in advance to avoid the queues outside the ticket office which are sometimes very long. *April–Sept daily 10am–7pm, Oct Mon–Fri 10am–6pm, Sat, Sun 10am–7pm, Nov–March Mon–Fri 10am–5pm, Sat, Sun 10am–7pm | entrance fee from 10.50 euros, children from 5.50 euros | Willi-Daume-Platz 1 | www.visitsealife.com | U 3 Olympiazentrum*

TIERPARK HELLABRUNN
(137 D3) (∅ G12)

Feed the fallow deer in the children's section of the more than 100-year-old zoo, stroke the miniature goats or take a ride on a camel. Find out about feeding times in advance! The animal shows, held every day, such as the elephants' jungle patrol or the birds of prey being taught to hunt, are fascinating. *April–Sept 8am–6pm, Oct–March 9am–5pm | entrance fee 11 euros, children 4.50 euros | Tierparkstraße 30 | www.tierpark-hellabrunn.de | U3 Thalkirchen*

VOLKSSTERNWARTE
(135 E4) (∅ L9)

On a clear evening you and your children can look at the far-off planets in the observatory, watch the International Space Station as it orbits the earth and, sometimes, even listen to the astronauts' radio messages. Every Friday there is an afternoon tour for children (5pm). *Mon–Fri Sept–March 8pm–10pm, April–Aug 9pm–11pm | entrance fee 5 euros, children 3 euros | Rosenheimer Straße 145 h | www.sternwarte-muenchen.de | U2 Karl-Preis-Platz*

FESTIVALS & EVENTS

The festival agenda has strong traditional roots and two major highlights which both have something to do with beer: the so-called 'fifth season', when potent bock beer is tapped and, of course, the world-famous Oktoberfest. While the former is a more intimate Munich affair, the latter is when Munich hosts the world.

PUBLIC HOLIDAYS

1 Jan New Year's Day, **6 Jan** Epiphany, **Good Friday, Easter Monday, 1 May** Labour Day, **Ascension Day, Whit Monday, Corpus Christi, 15 Aug** Assumption, **3 Oct** Day of German Unity, **1 Nov** All Saints, **25/26 Dec.** There are also 3 half-day holidays, introduced to keep everyone happy: shops close at noon not only on Christmas Eve and New Year's Eve but also on Fasching Tuesday.

FESTIVALS & EVENTS

JANUARY/FEBRUARY

▶ *Fasching:* From Thu–Tue there's lots going on. The highlight has to be the dance of the (female) stall holders on the Viktualienmarkt on Fasching Tuesday. Every 7 years (2012, 2019), the legendary 'Schäffler' (Coopers') Dance, which encouraged the locals to start having fun again after the Plague in the 16th century, is performed

MARCH/APRIL

▶ *Krimifestival:* Crime writers from all over the world hold readings in unusual places such as the police headquarters. *www.krimifestival-muenchen.de*
▶ *Starkbier time:* 2 weeks from Ash Wednesday until Easter; started by Paulaner monks in 1651 who decided that fasting was better if you could still drink beer. Since then, all major breweries in Bavaria produce their own 'doppelbocks'.
▶ *Easter egg hunt in the zoo:* Easter Sunday/Monday.
▶ *Frühlingsfest:* Mini Oktoberfest on the Theresienwiese at the end of April.

APRIL/JULY/OCTOBER

▶ INSIDER TIP *Auer Dult:* Munich's largest flea market held on Mariahilfplatz three times a year for nine days at a time: from the Sat before 1 May, from St Jacob's Day onwards in July and from the 3rd Sat in Oct. *www.auerdult.de*

The 'fifth season', festivals, concerts – and the biggest hangover in the world: the people of Munich know how to have fun

MAY

▶ *Dokumentarfilmfestival:* Germany's most important film festival of its kind. For 1 week all eyes are focussed on the Film Museum. *(St.-Jakobs-Platz 1 | tel. 089 23 32 48 88 | www.dokfest-muenchen.de)*

JUNE–AUGUST

▶ *Opernfestspiele:* Opera Festival in June and July; ticket office for advance bookings opens at the end of Jan. *(Bayerische Staatsoper | tel. 089 21 85 19 20 | www. muenchner-opern-festspiele.de)*

▶ *Tollwood-Sommerfestival:* 3 weeks in July at the Olympic Park (south); musical and theatrical events. *(Tickets: tel. (*) 0700 38 38 50 24 or www.tollwood.de)*

▶ *Münchner Filmfest* in June/July: Directors from around the world show what is new in the film industry. Parties with stars in the evenings. Tickets: *www. filmfest-muenchen.de*

▶ INSIDER TIP ● *impark Sommerfestival:* In July and August – one of the highlights of the open-air season in the Olympiapark, with live concerts and fairground rides. Entrance free! *www.impark.de*

SEPTEMBER/OCTOBER

▶ ★ *Oktoberfest:* Beer festival and funfair stretching over three weekends, the last being the first weekend in October. Traditional opening ceremony, when the Lord Mayor of Munich taps the first keg of beer, takes place at noon in the Schottenhamel tent on the first Sat. *www. oktoberfest.de/en*

NOVEMBER/DECEMBER

▶ *Tollwood-Winterfestival:* Munich's prettiest Christmas Market held on the Theresienwiese backed up by a superb progamme of cultural events (until 31 Dec). *www.tollwood.de*

LINKS, BLOGS, APPS & MORE

LINKS

▶ www.ehow.com/how_7846431_learn-bavarian-german Being able to speak German may be one thing, but will you be able to cope with Bavarian? The locals are very proud of their dialect and you'll hear it everywhere – from the more gentle lilt in Munich to the hardcore accent in the mountains

▶ www.oktoberfest.de/en Everything you need to know about the largest folk festival in the world, with horoscope, Oktoberfest shop, live cams and a flirt test

▶ www.nachtagenten.de Famous and comprehensive nightlife portal, first started in Munich, providing essential information on parties and events in its native city. Although in German, times, places and events are self explanatory

▶ www.m-360.de Virtual tour through the city with 360° panoramic pictures of some 70 major sites

▶ www.memoryloops.net Munich has its dark sides too. This detailed and fascinating site deals with places where Nazi terror was perpetrated within the city boundaries. 300 audio tracks with authentic contemporary witness reports

▶ http://travel.yahoo.com/p-map-191501749-map_of_munich_by-i Interactive map with useful tourist information and user reviews

BLOGS & FORUMS

▶ www.travelblog.org/Europe/Germany/Bavaria/Munich Blogs, photos, tips and forums on and of Munich by fellow tourists

▶ www.expat-blog.com/en/directory/europe/germany/munich Expats tell their tales of living in the Bavarian capital, plus all sorts of information and useful tips for those intending to spend some time here too

▶ http://bayern.theoffside.com football fans meet up on this site which is packed with reports, comments and links to make any footie-fan's heart beat faster

Regardless of whether you are still preparing your trip or already in Munich: these addresses will provide you with more information, videos and networks to make your holiday even more enjoyable

▶ www.munichphotoblog.com A blog with a difference – artistic and atmospheric photographs of everyday Munich. Quality images which capture many an undisturbed corner of the city, far from the glossy, over-restored tourist areas

▶ www.destination-munich.com/about-the-author.html An Aussie's view of Munich, having fallen in love with the place and explored pretty much everything and everywhere. Can't get much more comprehensive information than here. 'Munich grows on you,' as he writes 'like a beer belly or a big, curly moustache'

▶ www.monacomedia.de/muenchenwiki/index.php/Webcams Live web cams of all sorts of places in Munich

▶ www.wiesn-gaudi.tv The first 'social media' programme broadcasting live from the Oktoberfest. Amusing videos for beer fans and others, even if only in German

▶ www.oktoberfest.de/en/article/Visit+Munich/Getting+there/Useful+iPhone +Apps+for+your+visit/1744 New iPhone app subdivided into three sections: sights, restaurants, bars & clubs; especially suitable for short weekend trips to Munich

▶ www.qmapps.com/?category_name=munich-subway Makes getting around Munich all that much easier

▶ itunes.apple.com/us/app/munich-guide-mtrip/id389779181?mt=8 Intelligently presented travel guide with extensive directory of places to visit, customisable and automated trip itineraries, maps and navigation

▶ www.couchsurfing.org For couch potatoes happy to lounge around but who want to get to know Munich with those with first-hand experience

▶ www.facebook.com/groupon.muenchen Although in German, this network gives the cash-strapped tourist or those wanting to save some money information about discounts (up to 80%), updated daily, in restaurants, sport and spa facilities, etc.

TRAVEL TIPS

ARRIVAL

✈ Munich international airport is located 28.5km (17¾mi) northeast of the city. The main information stand at the airport is in the central terminal area (Zentralbereich) *(tel. 089 9 75 00)* from where there is direct access to the S-Bahn lines S1 (via Laim) and S 8 (via the Ostbahnhof) to the city centre every 20 mins. Single tickets cost just under 11 euros or 9.60 if you buy a 'stripe ticket' (Streifenkarte). Taxis cost around 60 euros. Your should reckon with a journey of at least 35 mins. to the main station. Buses run from the city centre to the airport every day from 5.10am–7.50pm, roughly every 20 mins.; from the airport to the city centre from 6.20am–9.40pm. Price: 10.50 euros.

🚗 The motorways from Nuremberg, Salzburg, Garmisch-Partenkirchen and Lindau filter into the ring road (Mittlerer Ring); the Stuttgart motorway merges into Verdistraße in the northwest. There are some 35 park-and-ride carparks at underground and suburban stations on the edge of the city and towards the airport *(www.parkundride.de)*.

🚆 Pasing in the west and the Ostbahnhof in the east are transit stations; the main station is in the middle of the city with connections to virtually all underground and suburban (U/S-Bahn) lines. Information: *tel. (*) 0180 599 66 33 | www.bahn.de*

BICYCLE HIRE

RADIUS TOURISTIK
(136 C4) *(𝄞 G7)* | *in the main station opposite track 32 | tel. 089 59 6113 | mid April–Oct daily 9am–6pm | 3 euros an hour, 14.50 euros a day*

CALL A BIKE
Call a Bike has around 2000 bikes around the city. They can be unlocked by entering a code. Bikes can be left anywhere. Payment is by credit card or direct debit. Basic price: 8 cents/min., max. 9 euros/day. *Tel. (*) 07000 5 22 55 22 | www.callabike.de*

CAMPING

THALKIRCHEN
Next to the Isar in a landscape conservation area. (136 C4) *(𝄞 F12)* | *Zentralländestr. 49 | tel. 089 7 23 17 07 | 15 March–31 Oct | U 3 Thalkirchen, then bus 135 or a 10 min. walk*

OBERMENZING
(0) *(𝄞 0)* | *Lochhausener Str. 59 | tel. 089 8 11 22 35 | 15 March–31 Oct S 2 Untermenzing, bus 164*

From arrival to weather

Holiday from start to finish: the most important addresses and information for your Munich trip

CONSULATES

BRITISH CONSULATE GENERAL
Möhlstraße 5 | 81675 München | tel. +49 89 21 10 90 | ukingermany.fco.gov.uk/en

US CONSULATE GENERAL
Königinstraße 5 | 80539 München | tel. +49 89 28 88-0 | munich.usconsulate.gov

CUSTOMS

EU citizens may import and export goods for their own personal use tax-free. Duty-free for non-EU citizens are: 50g perfume, 2L wine, 1L spirits and 200 cigarettes.

EMERGENCY SERVICES

Police: *tel. 110,* fire brigade and ambulance: *112,* on-call doctor (*): *01805 19 12 12,* emergency dental service: *089 7 23 30 93,* emergency number in case of poisoning: *192 40.*

GUIDED TOURS & SIGHTSEEING TOURS

Most bus tours of Munich leave from the *Bahnhofsplatz* outside the station between Karstadt and Elisenhof (126 A3) (*Ø G7*). These include *Munich sightseeing tours* in ● red double-deckers *(www.citysightseeing-muenchen.de)* and ● blue double-deckers run by the *Sightseeing Gray Line (www.stadtrundfahrten-muenchen.de).* The 1–2 hour 'hop on hop off' tours cost 10–19 euros. INSIDER TIP Online tickets for the red double-decker are up to 4 euros cheaper. The variety of tours offered by the blue line is more extensive. A cheaper alternative is to take a ● *tram* that runs past a lot of sights. Line 18 travels east-

BUDGETING

Coffee	£2–£2.50/$3–$3.50	
	for a cup of coffee	
Beer	£2.50–£3/$3.50–$4.50	
	for half a litre	
Dirndl	from £95/$145	
	incl. apron and blouse	
Food	£6.50–£12/$10–$18.50	
	for lunch	
Cinema	£3.50–£5.50/	
	$5.50–$8.50	
	on Mon and Tue	

west from Effnerplatz, crosses the Isar and trundles past the English Garden to Isartor and through the city centre, before continuing into the heart of trendy Westend. Tram no. 16 starts in St Emmeram, passes Effnerplatz and the Maximilianeum – the Bavarian parliament – and the Deutsches Museum, ending at Romanplatz not far from Nymphenburg Palace in the west. If you want to discover the not so well-known attractions of the Bavarian capital, take a guided walking tour through the centre with *Weis(s)en Stadtvogel München (www.weisser-stadtvogel.de).* Interesting alternatives are the 90 min. 'Shops & Shopping' tour *(18 euros)* or the 'Taste of Viktualienmarkt' tour *(21 euros). Stattreisen Munich (www.stattreisen-muenchen.de)* offers more than 80 tours with different themes ranging from 'Green and ecological Munich' to 'Tradition' *(each 9 euros).* On *Marienplatz* (127 D4) (*Ø H–J7*), a number of ● rickshaws *(www.muenchen-rikscha.de)* stand ready for visitors. These personal tours (30–90 mins.) are more expensive *(35–75 euros).*

CURRENCY CONVERTER

£	€	€	£
1	1.30	1	0.80
3	3.80	3	2.40
5	6.30	5	4
13	16.30	13	10
40	50	40	32
75	94	75	60
120	150	120	96
250	313	250	200
500	625	500	400

$	€	€	$
1	0.80	1	1.20
3	2.50	3	3.60
5	4.20	5	6
13	11	13	15.50
40	33	40	48
75	62.50	75	90
120	100	120	144
250	208	250	300
500	417	500	600

For current exchange rates see www.xe.com

Technology fans shouldn't miss out on the 50-min. tour of *Franz-Josef-Strauss Airport (9 euros |* (139 D2) *(*𝄞 *O) | only with advance reservation: tel. 089 97 54 13 33 | www.munich-airport.de)*. The *Münchner Bildungswerk (tel. 089 545 80 50 | www. muenchner-bildungswerk.de)* is specialised in church tours which provide in-depth information on the history and architecture. Other variations include brewery tours, such as the 3–4 hour 'Spaten-Franziskaner Brewery Tour' *(13.80 euros |* (133 E1) *(*𝄞 *F6) | Marsstr. 46/48 | only with advance reservation: tel. 089 52 00 22 45 | www.spatenbraeu.de)*, and ● football tours *(from 49.90 euros | tel. 089 41 35 36 61 | www.stadion-tours.de)* on Sat and Sun to places where football history was written, followed by a tour of the *stadium on Schleißheimer Straße* (→ p. 88).

INFORMATION

TOURIST INFORMATION OFFICE
(127 D4) *(*𝄞 *G7) | Sendlinger Str. 1 | tel. information: 089 23 39 65 00 | www. muenchen-tourist.de*

MAIN STATION
(126 A3) *(*𝄞 *G7) | Mon–Sat 9am–8pm, Sun 10am–4pm, may vary according to season | Bahnhofplatz 2, to the right of the main entrance*

MARIENPLATZ
(126 D4) *(*𝄞 *H7) | Mon–Fri 10am–8pm, Sat 10am–4pm, may vary according to season | in the Neues Rathaus*

INTERNET

www.muenchen.de, the city's official portal, provides valuable information on travel, culture and city services; *www.muenchen-online.de* has pictures from the city's webcams; *www.munichx.de* has useful nightlife and restaurants tips; *www.in-muenchen.de*, a free events magazine's online portal, has details of concerts, films, theatre performances and exhibitions; *www.ganz-muenchen.de*, lists masses of regular events, such as flea markets and festivals, as well as up-to-the-minute events; *www. prinz.de/muenchen* tells you what parties are being held where; *www.meinestadt.de/ muenchen* has lots of information – from the weather to a map and hotel addresses.

INTERNET CAFÉS & WIFI

There are dozens of internet cafés. Ones in the centre include *Internetcafé München* on the lower level of the main station

(Mon–Fri 8am–11pm, Sat, Sun 9am–11pm | (126 A3) (ØØ G7) | Bahnhofsplatz 2). Many cafés and hotels also have WiFi. A pleasant place to surf is *Tagträumer (Mon–Fri 8am–7.30pm, Sat, Sun 10am–7pm | (134 A4) (ØØ G9) | Dreimühlenstr. 17)* and *Hoover & Floyd (Mon–Fri 8am–1am, Sat, Sun 10am–1am | (134 B3) (ØØ H8) | Ickstattstr. 2).* Just ask for the access data and off you go. Easy surfing is also available in branches of *Starbucks* and *Coffee-Fellows*.

PUBLIC TRANSPORT

Underground and suburban trains (U and S-Bahn) run every 5 or 10 mins. from 7am–7pm, before or after that at least every 20 mins. At night, buses and trams operate a reduced service (Sun–Thu every 60 mins., Fri, Sat every 30 mins.). Ticket machines can be found in every station and in buses and trams. Many accept cards. The MVV (Munich transport company) network is divided into 4 concentric zones from the centre to the outskirts. The more zones you enter or cross the higher the price. In the central zone, where most sights are located, the following fares apply – single journey: 2.50 euros; day pass for an unlimited number of journeys: 5.40 euros; partner day pass (valid for up to 5 adults): 9.80 euros. Tickets must be validated before getting on. Combined tickets are available for attractions outside the city which include admission and the cost of the journey – e.g. for the Therme Erding (a spa/bathing oasis) or for Sea Life (→ p. 109). *Information: 41 42 43 44 | www.mvv-muenchen.de*

TAXI

Basic price 3.30 euros, plus between 1.40 and 1.70 euros per kilometre. Central tel. no.: *tel. 194 10 | www.taxi-muenchen.com*

WEATHER IN MUNICH

	Jan	Feb	March	April	May	June	July	Aug	Sept	Oct	Nov	Dec
Daytime temperatures in °C/°F	1/34	3/37	9/48	14/57	18/64	21/70	23/73	23/73	20/68	13/55	7/45	2/36
Nighttime temperatures in °C/°F	−6/21	−5/23	−2/28	3/37	7/45	10/50	12/54	11/52	8/46	4/39	0/32	−4/25
Sunshine hours/day	2	3	5	6	7	7	7	7	6	4	2	1
Precipitation days/month	11	10	9	10	12	14	13	12	10	9	9	10

USEFUL PHRASES GERMAN

PRONUNCIATION

We have provided a simple pronunciation aid for German words
(see the square brackets). Note the following:

ch	usually like ch in Scottish "loch", shown here as [kh]
g	hard as in "get"
ß	is a double s
ä	like the vowel in "fair" or "bear"
ö	a little like er as in "her"
ü	is spoken as oo with rounded lips, like the French "tu"
ie	is ee as in "fee", but ei is like "height", shown here as [ei]
'	stress on the following syllable

IN BRIEF

Yes/No/Maybe	Ja [yah]/Nein [nein]/Vielleicht [fee'leikht]
Please/Thank you	Bitte ['bi-te]/Danke ['dan-ke]
Sorry	Entschuldige [ent'shul-di-ge]
Excuse me, please	Entschuldigen Sie [ent'shul-di-gen zee]
May I ...?/ Pardon?	Darf ich ...? [darf ikh]/Wie bitte? [vee 'bi-te]
I would like to .../ have you got ...?	Ich möchte ... [ikh 'merkh-te]/ Haben Sie ...? ['hab-en zee]
How much is ...?	Wie viel kostet ...? [vee-feel 'koss-tet]
I (don't) like this	Das gefällt mir/nicht [das ge-'felt meer/nikht]
good/bad	gut/schlecht [goot/shlekht]
broken/doesn't work	kaputt [ka-'put]/funktioniert nicht/ funk-tsion-'eert nikht]
too much/much/little	(zu) viel/wenig [tsoo feel/'vay-nikh]
Help!/Attention!/ Caution!	Hilfe! ['hil-fe]/Achtung! [akh-'tung]/ Vorsicht! ['for-sikht]
ambulance	Krankenwagen ['kran-ken-vaa-gen]/ Notarzt ['note-aatst]
police/fire brigade	Polizei [pol-i-'tsei]/Feuerwehr ['foy-er-vayr]
danger/dangerous	Gefahr [ge-'far]/gefährlich [ge-'fair-likh]

GREETINGS, FAREWELL

Good morning!/after-noon!/evening!/night!	Gute(n) Morgen ['goo-ten 'mor-gen]/Tag [taag]/ Abend ['aa-bent]/Nacht [nakht]
Hello!/goodbye!	Hallo ['ha-llo]/Auf Wiedersehen [owf 'vee-der-zayn]

Sprichst du Deutsch?

"Do you speak German?" This guide will help you to say the basic words and phrases in German.

See you!	Tschüss [chüss]
My name is ...	Ich heiße ... [ikh 'hei-sse]
What's your name?	Wie heißt Du [vee heist doo]/ heißen Sie? ['heiss-en zee]
I'm from ...	Ich komme aus ... [ikh 'ko-mme ows]

DATE & TIME

Monday/Tuesday	Montag ['moan-tag]/Dienstag ['deens-tag]
Wednesday/Thursday	Mittwoch ['mit-vokh]/Donnerstag ['don-ers-tag]
Friday/Saturday	Freitag ['frei-tag]/Samstag ['zams-tag]
Sunday/holiday	Sonntag ['zon-tag]/Feiertag ['fire-tag]
today/tomorrow/ yesterday	heute ['hoy-te]/morgen ['mor-gen]/ gestern ['gess-tern]
hour/minute	Stunde ['shtun-de]/Minute [min-'oo-te]
day/night/week	Tag [tag]/Nacht [nakht]/Woche ['vo-khe]
What time is it?	Wie viel Uhr ist es? ['vee-feel oor ist es]
It's three o'clock	Es ist drei Uhr [ez ist drei oor]

TRAVEL

open/closed	offen ['off-en]/geschlossen [ge-'shloss-en]
entrance (vehicles)	Zufahrt ['tsoo-faat]
entrance/exit	Eingang ['ein-gang]/Ausgang ['ows-gang]
arrival/departure (flight)	Ankunft ['an-kunft]/Abflug ['ap-floog]
toilets/restrooms / ladies/gentlemen	Toiletten [twa-'let-en]/ Damen ['daa-men]/Herren ['her-en]
(no) drinking water	(kein) Trinkwasser [(kein) 'trink-vass-er]
Where is ...?/Where are ...?	Wo ist ...? [vo ist]/Wo sind ...? [vo zint]
left/right	links [links]/rechts [rekhts]
straight ahead/back	geradeaus [ge-raa-de-'ows]/zurück [tsoo-'rük]
close/far	nah [naa]/weit [veit]
taxi/cab	Taxi ['tak-si]
bus stop/ cab stand	Bushaltestelle [bus-hal-te-'shtell-e]/ Taxistand ['tak-si- shtant]
parking lot/parking garage	Parkplatz ['park-plats]/Parkhaus ['park-hows]
street map/map	Stadtplan ['shtat-plan]/Landkarte ['lant-kaa-te]
airport/train station	Flughafen ['floog-ha-fen]/ Bahnhof ['baan-hoaf]
schedule/ticket	Fahrplan ['faa-plan]/Fahrschein ['faa-shein]
I would like to rent ...	Ich möchte ... mieten [ikh 'mer-khte ... 'mee-ten]
a car/a bicycle	ein Auto [ein 'ow-to]/ein Fahrrad [ein 'faa-raat]
a motorhome/RV	ein Wohnmobil [ein 'vone-mo-beel]
a boat	ein Boot [ein 'boat]

petrol/gas station	Tankstelle ['tank-shtell-e]
petrol/gas / diesel	Benzin [ben-'tseen]/Diesel ['dee-zel]
breakdown/repair shop	Panne ['pan-e]/Werkstatt ['verk-shtat]

FOOD & DRINK

Could you please book a table for tonight for four?	Reservieren Sie uns bitte für heute Abend einen Tisch für vier Personen [rez-er-'vee-ren zee uns 'bi-te für 'hoy-te 'aa-bent 'ein-en tish für feer pair-'zo-nen]
The menu, please	Die Speisekarte, bitte [dee 'shpei-ze-kaa-te 'bi-te]
Could I please have ...?	Könnte ich ... haben? ['kern-te ikh ... 'haa-ben]
with/without ice/ sparkling	mit [mit]/ohne Eis ['oh-ne eis]/ Kohlensäure ['koh-len-zoy-re]
vegetarian/allergy	Vegetarier(in) [veg-e-'taa-ree-er]/Allergie [al-air-'gee]
May I have the bill, please?	Ich möchte zahlen, bitte [ikh 'merkh-te 'tsaa-len 'bi-te]

SHOPPING

Where can I find...?	Wo finde ich ...? [vo 'fin-de ikh]
I'd like .../I'm looking for ...	Ich möchte ... [ikh 'merkh-te]/Ich suche ... [ikh 'zoo-khe]
pharmacy/chemist	Apotheke [a-po-'tay-ke]/Drogerie [dro-ge-'ree]
shopping centre	Einkaufszentrum [ein-kowfs-'tsen-trum]
expensive/cheap/price	teuer ['toy-er]/billig ['bil-ig]/Preis [preis]
more/less	mehr [mayr]/weniger ['vay-ni-ger]
organically grown	aus biologischem Anbau [ows bee-o-'lo-gish-em 'an-bow]

ACCOMMODATION

I have booked a room	Ich habe ein Zimmer reserviert [ikh 'haa-be ein 'tsi-me rez-erv-'eert]
Do you have any ... left?	Haben Sie noch ein ... ['haa-ben zee nokh]
single room	Einzelzimmer ['ein-tsel-tsi-mer]
double room	Doppelzimmer ['dop-el-tsi-mer]
breakfast/half board	Frühstück ['frü-shtük]/Halbpension ['halp-pen-si-ohn]
full board	Vollpension ['foll-pen-si-ohn]
shower/sit-down bath	Dusche ['doo-she]/Bad [baat]
balcony/terrasse	Balkon [bal-'kohn]/Terrasse [te-'rass-e]
key/room card	Schlüssel ['shlü-sel]/Zimmerkarte ['tsi-mer-kaa-te]
luggage/suitcase	Gepäck [ge-'pek]/Koffer ['koff-er]/Tasche ['ta-she]

BANKS, MONEY & CREDIT CARDS

bank/ATM	Bank/Geldautomat [bank/'gelt-ow-to-maat]
pin code	Geheimzahl [ge-'heim-tsaal]
I'd like to change ...	Ich möchte ... wechseln [ikh 'merkh-te ... 'vek-seln]

| cash/credit card | bar [bar]/Kreditkarte [kre-'dit-kaa-te] |
| bill/coin | Banknote ['bank-noh-te]/Münze ['mün-tse] |

HEALTH

doctor/dentist/	Arzt [aatst]/Zahnarzt ['tsaan-aatst]/
paediatrician	Kinderarzt ['kin-der-aatst]
hospital/	Krankenhaus ['kran-ken-hows]/
emergency clinic	Notfallpraxis ['note-fal-prak-sis]
fever/pain	Fieber ['fee-ber]/Schmerzen ['shmer-tsen]
diarrhoea/nausea	Durchfall ['doorkh-fal]/Übelkeit ['ü-bel-keit]
inflamed/injured	entzündet [ent-'tsün-det]/verletzt [fer-'letst]
prescription	Rezept [re-'tsept]
pain reliever/tablet	Schmerzmittel ['shmerts-mit-el]/Tablette [ta-'blet-e]

POST, TELECOMMUNICATIONS & MEDIA

stamp/letter	Briefmarke ['brief-maa-ke]/Brief [brief]
postcard	Postkarte ['posst-kaa-te]
I'm looking for a prepaid card for my mobile	Ich suche eine Prepaid-Karte für mein Handy [ikh 'zoo-khe 'ei-ne 'pre-paid-kaa-te für mein 'hen-dee]
Do I need a special area code?	Brauche ich eine spezielle Vorwahl? ['brow-khe ikh 'ei-ne shpets-ee-'ell-e 'fore-vaal]
Where can I find internet access?	Wo finde ich einen Internetzugang? [vo 'fin-de ikh 'ei-nen 'in-ter-net-tsoo-gang]
socket/adapter/	Steckdose ['shtek-doh-ze]/Adapter [a-'dap-te]/
charger/wi-fi	Ladegerät ['laa-de-ge-rayt]/WLAN ['vay-laan]

LEISURE, SPORTS & BEACH

bike/scooter rental	Fahrrad-['faa-raat]/Mofa-Verleih ['mo-fa fer-lei]
rental shop	Vermietladen [fer-'meet-laa-den]
lesson	Übungsstunde ['ü-bungs-shtun-de]

NUMBERS

0 null [null]	10 zehn [tsayn]	20 zwanzig ['tsvantsikh]
1 eins [eins]	11 elf [elf]	50 Fünfzig ['fünf-tsikh]
2 zwei [tsvei]	12 zwölf [tsvölf]	100 (ein) Hundert ['hun-dert]
3 drei [drei]	13 dreizehn [' dreitsayn]	200 Zwei Hundert [tsvei 'hun-dert]
4 vier [feer]	14 vierzehn ['feertsayn]	1000 (ein) Tausend ['tow-zent]
5 fünf [fünf]	15 fünfzehn ['fünftsayn]	2000 Zwei Tausend [tsvei 'tow-zent]
6 sechs [zex]	16 sechzehn ['zekhtsayn]	10 000 Zehn Tausend [tsayn 'tow-zent]
7 sieben ['zeeben]	17 siebzehn ['zeebtsayn]	
8 acht [akht]	18 achtzehn ['akhtsayn]	½ ein halb [ein halp]
9 neun [noyn]	19 neunzehn ['noyntsayn]	¼ ein viertel [ein 'feer-tel]

NOTES

MARCO POLO TRAVEL GUIDES

ALGARVE
AMSTERDAM
ATHENS
AUSTRALIA
BANGKOK
BARCELONA
BERLIN
BRUSSELS
BUDAPEST
CALIFORNIA
CAMBODIA
CAPE TOWN
  WINE LANDS,
  GARDEN ROUTE
CHINA
COLOGNE
COPENHAGEN
CORFU
COSTA BLANCA
  VALENCIA
COSTA DEL SOL
  GRANADA
CRETE
CUBA

CYPRUS
  NORTH AND
  SOUTH
DUBAI
DUBLIN
DUBROVNIK &
  DALMATIAN COAST
EDINBURGH
EGYPT
FINLAND
FLORENCE
FLORIDA
FRENCH RIVIERA
  NICE, CANNES &
  MONACO
FUERTEVENTURA
GRAN CANARIA
HONG KONG
  MACAU
ICELAND
IRELAND
ISRAEL
ISTANBUL
JORDAN

KOS
KRAKOW
LAKE GARDA
LANZAROTE
LAS VEGAS
LISBON
LONDON
LOS ANGELES
MADEIRA
  PORTO SANTO
MADRID
MALLORCA
MALTA
  GOZO
MOROCCO
MUNICH
NEW YORK
NEW ZEALAND
NORWAY
OSLO
PARIS

PRAGUE
RHODES
ROME
SAN FRANCISCO
SARDINIA
SHANGHAI
SICILY
SOUTH AFRICA
STOCKHOLM
TENERIFE
THAILAND
TURKEY
TURKEY
  SOUTH COAST
TUSCANY
UNITED ARAB
  EMIRATES
VENICE
VIENNA
VIETNAM

- PACKED WITH INSIDER TIPS
- BEST WALKS AND TOURS
- FULL-COLOUR PULL-OUT MAP
  AND STREET ATLAS

STREET ATLAS

The green line ▬▬ indicates the Walking tours (p. 102–107)

All tours are also marked on the pull-out map

Photo: Nymphenburger Park

Exploring Munich

The map on the back cover shows how the area has been sub-divided

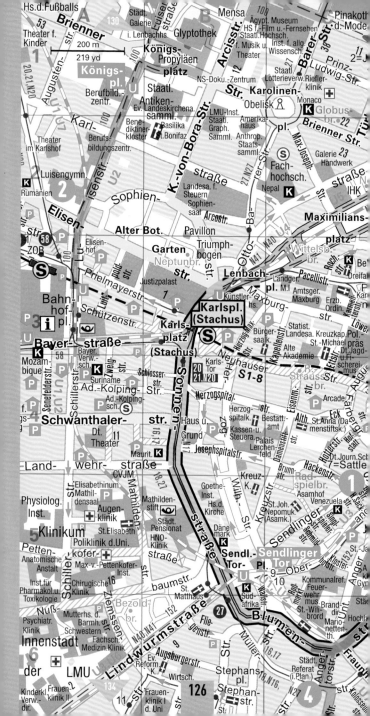

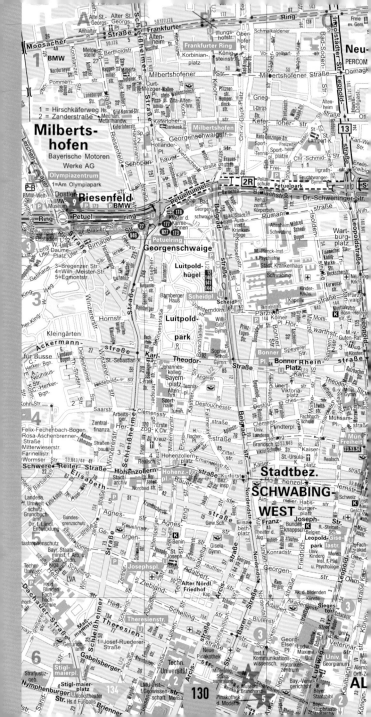

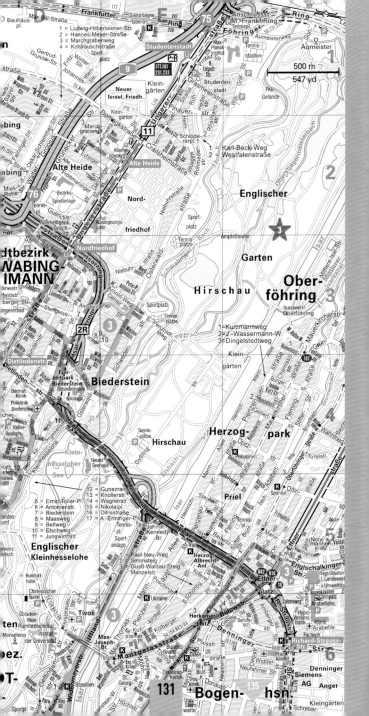

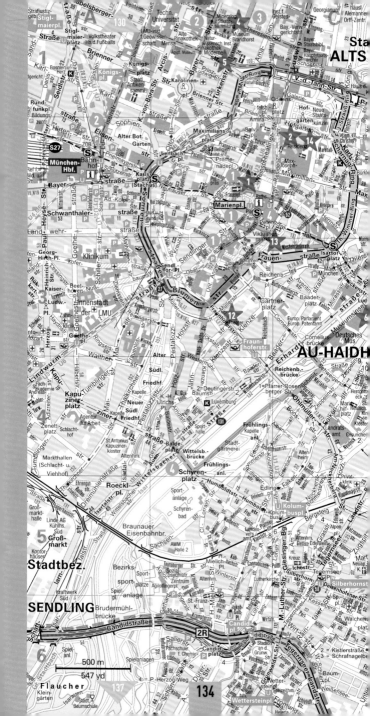

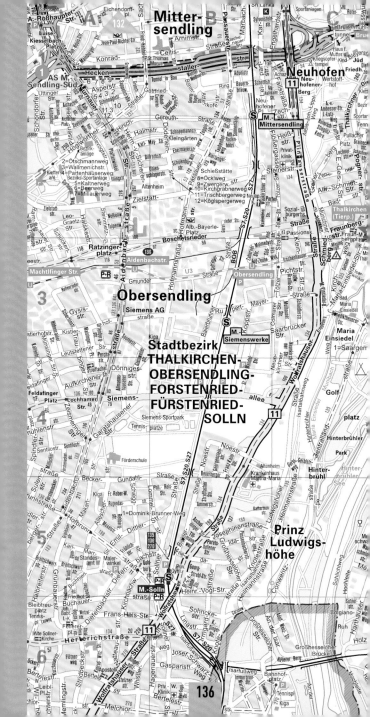

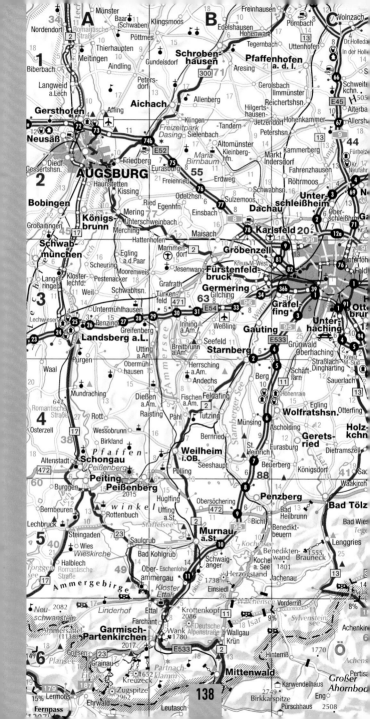

This index lists a selection of the streets and squares shown in the street atlas

A
Aberlestraße **133/E5**
Ackermannstraße **129/F4**
Adalbert-Stifter-Straße **131/F5**
Adalbertstraße **130/B5**
Adelgundenstraße **134/C2**
Adolf-Kolping-Straße
126/A4–133/F2
Agnes-Bernauer-Straße **132/B2**
Agnesstraße **129/F5**
Aidenbachstraße **136/A5**
Aindorferstraße **132/A3**
Ainmillerstraße **130/B5**
Akademiestraße **130/C6**
Albertgasse **127/D4**
Albert-Roßhaupter-Straße **132/C6**
Albrechtstraße **129/E5**
Alexandrastraße **135/D2**
Allacher Straße **128/A2**
Altenhofstraße **127/D4**
Alter Messeplatz **133/E3**
Altheimer Eck **126/C4–134/B2**
Am Einlaß **127/D5**
Am Gasteig **135/D3**
Am Gries **135/D1**
Am Harras **133/E5**
Am Isarkanal **136/C2**
Am Kosttor **127/E4**
Am Lilienberg **135/D3**
Am Nockherberg **134/C4**
Am Perlacher Forst **137/E4**
Am Westpark **133/D4**
Amalienstraße **127/D1**
Amiraplatz **127/D2**
Ampfingstraße **135/F4**
An der Hauptfeuerwache (10)
126/C5
Angertorstr. **126/C6**
Anglerstraße **133/D3**
Anzinger Straße **135/E4**
Arabellastraße **131/F6**
Arcisstraße **126/B1–130/B6**
Arcostraße **126/B2–134/B2**
Aretinstraße **137/D3**
Arnulfstraße **128/B6–133/D1**
Artur-Kutscher-Platz **131/D4**
Aschheimer Straße **135/F4**
Athener Platz **137/E4**
Auenstraße **134/B4**
Auerfeldstraße **135/D4**
Auf der Insel **134/C3**
Augsburgerstraße **126/B6–134/A3**
Augustenstraße **126/A1–134/A1**
Augustinerstraße **126/C4–134/B2**
Authariplatz **137/E3**
Aventinstraße **127/E5**

B
Baaderplatz **127/E6**
Baaderstraße **127/E6**
Bad-Schachener-Straße **135/F4**
Bahnhofplatz **126/A3–133/F2**
Balanstraße **135/D4**
Baldeplatz **134/B4**
Baldestraße **134/B4**
Baldurstraße **128/C4**
Barbarossastraße **135/F2**
Barer Straße **126/B2–134/B2**
Barthstraße **133/D2**
Baubergerstraße **128/A3**

Bauerstraße **130/B5**
Baumgartnerstraße **133/D4**
Bavariaring **133/E4**
Bavariastraße **133/E4**
Bayernplatz **130/B4**
Bayerstraße **126/A3–133/E2**
Beethovenplatz **133/F3**
Beethovenstraße **133/F3**
Belgradstraße **130/B2**
Berg-am-Laim-Straße **135/F3**
Bergmannstraße **133/D3**
Berliner Straße **130/C3**
Biedersteiner Straße **131/D4**
Birnauer Straße **129/F3**
Bismarckstraße **130/C4**
Blumenstraße **126/B6–134/B3**
Blutenburgstraße **129/D6**
Böhmerwaldplatz **135/F1**
Bonner Platz **130/C4**
Bonner Straße **130/C3**
Bordeauxplatz **135/D3**
Boschetsrieder Straße **136/B3**
Bräuhausstraße **127/E4**
Breisacher Straße **135/E3**
Brienner Straße **126/A1–130/A6**
Brudermühlbrücke **133/F6**
Brudermühlstraße **133/E6**
Bruderstraße **127/F2**
Bruggspergerstraße **137/E4**
Brundageplatz **129/F2**
Brunnerstraße **130/B3**
Brunnstraße **127/F2**
Bülowstraße **131/E6**
Bürgerstraße **131/F4**
Burgstraße **127/D4**
Bürkleinstraße **127/F3**
Buschingstraße **135/F1**
Buttermelcherstraße **127/D6**

C
Camerloherstraße **132/A3**
Candidplatz **134/B6**
Candidstraße **133/F6**
Christophstraße **127/E4**
Claude-Lorrain-Straße **134/B5**
Claudius-Keller-Straße **135/E5**
Clemensstraße **130/A4**
Corneliusbrücke **127/E6**
Corneliusstraße **127/D6**
Crailsheimstraße **131/E2**
Crusiusstraße (2) **135/D1**

D
Dachauer Straße **130/A6**
Daiserstraße **133/E5**
Damenstiftstraße **126/C4–134/B2**
Danklstraße **133/E5**
Dantestraße **128/C3**
Danziger Straße **131/D3**
Deisenhofener Straße **134/C5**
Delpstraße **131/F6**
Demollstraße **128/C4**
Denninger Straße **131/E6**
Destouchesstraße **130/B4**
Dianastraße **131/D6**
Dienerstraße **127/D4**
Dietlindenstraße **131/D4**
Dietramszeller Straße **133/E6**
Dom-Pedro-Platz **129/D5**
Dom-Pedro-Straße **129/D5**

Donnersbergerbrücke **133/D2**
Dornbergstraße **135/F4**
Dreifaltigkeitsplatz **127/E5**
Dreimühlenstraße **133/F5**
Drückeberger-Gassl (Viscardigasse)
127/D3
Dultstraße **126/C5**
Dürnbräugasse **127/E4**

E
Edlingerplatz **134/B5**
Eduard-Schmid-Straße **134/B4**
Effnerplatz **131/F5**
Effnerstraße **131/F5**
Eggernstraße **135/D3**
Ehrwalder Straße **132/B5**
Einsteinstraße **135/D2**
Eintrachtstraße **135/D5**
Eisenmannstraße **126/C4–134/B2**
Elisabethplatz **130/B5**
Elisabethstraße **129/F4**
Elisenstraße **126/A2–133/F2**
Elsässer Straße **135/E3**
Elsenheimerstraße **132/C2**
Elvirastraße **129/E6**
Emil-Riedel-Straße **131/D6**
Englschalkinger Straße **131/F5**
Enhuberstraße **130/B6**
Erhardtstraße **127/F6**
Erich-Kästner-Straße **130/B4**
Erich-Mühsam-Platz **130/C4**
Erzgießereistraße **129/F6**
Esperantoplatz **133/F3**
Ettstraße **126/C4–134/B2**
Europaplatz **135/D2**

F
Fachnerstraße **132/B3**
Falckenbergstraße **127/E3**
Falkenstraße **134/C5**
Falkenturmstraße **127/E3**
Fallmerayerstraße **130/B4**
Färbergraben **126/C4–134/B2**
Feilitzschstraße **130/C4**
Feldafinger Platz **136/A4**
Feldmochinger Straße **128/C2**
Fernpaßstraße **132/C5**
Filserbräugasse (6) **127/D4**
Finkenstraße **127/D2**
Flemingstraße **131/F5**
Fliegenstraße **126/B6**
Fliegenstraße **134/B3**
Flurstraße **135/E3**
Föhringer Ring **131/E1**
Frankfurter Ring **130/B1**
Franziskanerstraße **135/D4**
Franz-Josef-Strauß-Ring **127/F2**
Franz-Joseph-Straße **130/B5**
Franz-Mader-Straße **128/A3**
Frauenlobstraße **134/A4**
Frauenplatz **127/D4**
Frauenstraße **127/D5**
Fraunbergstraße **136/C2**
Fraunhoferstraße **126/C6–134/B3**
Friedenheimer Brücke **132/C2**
Friedenheimer Straße **132/B4**
Friedenstraße **135/E4**
Friedrichstraße **130/C5**
Fromundstraße **134/C6**
Führichstraße **135/F5**

Fürstenfelderstraße **126/C4**
Fürstenrieder Straße **132/A6**
Fürstenstraße **127/D1**

G
Gabelsbergerstraße **130/A6**
Galeriestraße **127/E2**
Galileiplatz **135/E1**
Ganghoferbrücke **133/D4**
Ganghoferstraße **133/E4**
Garmischer Straße **132/C4**
Gärtnerplatz **127/D6**
Gebsattelstraße **134/C4**
Gedonstraße **130/C5**
Geiselgasteigstraße **137/D6**
Georg-Brauchle-Ring **128/C2**
Georg-Elser-Platz **130/C6**
Georgenstraße **129/F5**
Georg-Freundorfer-Platz **133/D3**
Georg-Hirth-Platz **133/F3**
Germaniastraße **130/C4**
Geroltstraße **133/D3**
Geschwister-Scholl-Platz **130/C6**
Gewürzmühlstraße **134/C2**
Giesinger Berg **134/C5**
Giselastraße **130/C5**
Glückstraße **127/D1**
Goetheplatz **133/F3**
Goethestraße **133/F3**
Gollierplatz **133/D3**
Gollierstraße **133/D3**
Görresstraße **129/F5**
Gotthardstraße **132/A3**
Grafinger Straße **135/E4**
Grasserstraße **133/E2**
Grillparzerstraße **135/E2**
Gröbenzeller Straße **128/A2**
Grünwalder Straße **134/B6**
Grünwalder Straße **137/D4**
Grütznerstraße **135/D2**
Guardinistraße **132/A5**
Guido-Schneble-Straße **132/A4**

H
Habsburgerplatz **130/C5**
Hackenstraße **126/C4–134/B2**
Hackerbrücke **133/E2**
Hahnenstraße **127/E1**
Haidenauplatz **135/E3**
Haimhauserstraße **130/C4**
Hanauer Straße **129/D2**
Hansastraße **132/C3**
Hans-Fischer-Straße **133/E4**
Hans-Preißinger-Straße **137/D1**
Hans-Sachs-Straße **134/B3**
Harlachinger Berg **137/D3**
Harthauser Straße **136/C6**
Hartmannshofer Straße **128/A3**
Hartmannstraße **126/C3**
Haydnstraße **133/F3**
Heckenstallerstraße **132/C6**
Heiliggeiststraße **127/E4**
Heimeranplatz **133/E2**
Heimeranstraße **133/D3**
Helmut-Fischer-Platz **130/B4**
Herkomerplatz **131/E6**
Hermann-Sack-Straße **126/C5**
Herrnstraße **127/E4**
Herterichstraße **136/A6**
Herzog-Ernst-Platz **133/E4**
Herzog-Heinrich-Straße **133/F3**

Herzog-Max-Straße **126/B3–134/B2**
Herzog-Rudolf-Straße **127/F3**
Herzogspitalstraße **126/B4–134/A2**
Herzogstraße **130/A4**
Herzog-Wilhelm-Straße **126/B4–134/B2**
Heßstraße **129/E5**
Hildegardstraße **127/E4**
Hiltenspergerstraße **130/B5**
Himbselstraße **135/D1**
Himmelreichstraße **131/D6**
Hinterbärenbadstraße **132/C5**
Hirschgartenallee **128/B5**
Hochbrückenstraße **127/E4**
Hochstraße **134/C5**
Hochstraße **135/D3**
Hofgartenstraße **127/E2**
Hofgraben **127/E3**
Hofmannstraße **136/B3**
Hofstatt **126/C4**
Hogenbergplatz **132/B3**
Hohenlohestraße **129/D4**
Hohenzollernplatz **130/B4**
Hohenzollernstraße **130/A4**
Holbeinstraße **135/E1**
Holzhofstraße **135/D3**
Holzstraße **126/C6–134/B3**
Horemannstraße **129/D6**
Hörwarthstraße **130/C3**
Hotterstraße **126/C4–134/B2**
Hübnerstraße **129/D5**
Hugo-Troendle-Straße **128/B3**
Humboldtstraße **134/B5**

I
Ichostraße **134/C5**
Ickstattstraße **134/B3**
Ifflandstraße **131/D6**
Implerstraße **133/E4**
In den Kirschen **128/A3**
Infanteriestraße **129/F4**
Ingolstädter Straße **130/C1**
Innere Wiener Straße **135/D3**
Innsbrucker Ring **135/F3**
Isabellastraße **130/B5**
Isarring **131/D3**
Isartalstraße **133/F6**
Isartorplatz **127/E5**
Isenschmidtstraße **137/D4**
Ismaninger Straße **135/D2**
Isoldenstraße **130/C2**

J
Jägerstraße **127/D1**
Jahnstraße **134/B3**
Joergstraße **132/A4**
Johannisplatz **135/D3**
John-F.-Kennedy-Brücke **131/E5**
Josephspitalstraße **126/B4–134/A2**
Josephsplatz **130/B5**
Jungfernturmstraße (2) **126/C1**

K
Kaiser-Ludwig-Platz **133/F3**
Kaiserplatz **130/C4**
Kaiserstraße **130/B4**
Kanalstraße **127/F5**
Kapellenstraße **126/C4–134/B2**
Kapuzinerplatz **133/F4**
Kapuzinerstraße **133/F4**
Kardinal-Döpfner-Straße **127/D2**

Kardinal-Faulhaber-Straße **127/D3**
Karl-Müller-Weg **134/C3**
Karl-Preis-Platz **135/E5**
Karl-Scharnagl-Ring **127/F3**
Karlsplatz (Stachus) **126/B3–134/A2**
Karlstraße **129/F6**
Karl-Theodor-Straße **129/F3**
Karmeliterstraße **126/C3**
Karneidplatz **127/E5**
Karolinenplatz **126/B1–134/B1**
Karolinenstraße **131/D6**
Karolingerallee **137/D3**
Karwendelstraße **133/D6**
Katharina-von-Bora-Straße **126/B2**
Kaufingerstraße (3) **126/C4**
Kaulbachstraße **130/C6**
Kazmairstraße **133/D3**
Kellerstraße **135/D3**
Kidlerstraße **133/E5**
Kirchenstraße **135/D3**
Kirchseeoner Straße **135/F5**
Kißkaltplatz **130/C5**
Klarastraße **133/E1**
Klausener Straße **137/F2**
Klenzestraße **127/E6**
Klosterhofstraße **126/C5**
Klugstraße **128/C4**
Knöbelstraße **127/F4**
Kohlstraße **127/E6**
Kölner Platz **130/C3**
Kolosseumstraße **126/C6**
Kolumbusplatz **134/B5**
Kolumbusstraße **134/B4**
Königinstraße **127/F1**
Königsplatz **126/A1–134/A1**
Kraepelinstraße **130/B2**
Kreppeberg **136/C3**
Kreuzstraße **126/B5–134/B3**
Krüner Platz **132/B5**
Krüner Straße **132/B5**
Küchelbäckerstraße (13) **127/E5**
Kufsteiner Platz **131/E6**
Kuglmüllerstraße **128/B5**
Kunigundenstraße **131/D4**
Kurfürstenplatz **130/B4**
Kurfürstenstraße **130/B5**

L
Lachnerstraße **128/C6**
Laimer Platz **132/A3**
Lamontstraße **135/E2**
Landsberger Straße **133/E2**
Landschaftstraße **127/D4**
Landshuter Allee **129/E2**
Ländstraße **127/F5**
Landwehrstraße **133/F2**
Laurinplatz **137/E4**
Lautensackstraße **132/C3**
Lazarettstraße **129/E6**
Ledererstraße **127/E4**
Lenbachplatz **126/B3–134/B1**
Leonhard-Moll-Bogen **133/D3**
Leonrodplatz **129/E5**
Leonrodstraße **129/D6**
Leopoldstraße **130/C5**
Lerchenauer Straße **129/F2**
Lerchenfeldstraße **135/D1**
Leuchtenbergring **135/F2**
Liebfrauenstraße (4) **126/C4**
Liebherrstraße **127/F5**
Liebigstraße **134/C2**

Lilienstraße **134/C4**
Lindenstraße **137/D4**
Lindwurmstraße **133/E5**
Lothstraße **129/E6**
Löwengrube **126/C3–134/B2**
Lucile-Grahn-Straße **135/E2**
Ludwigsbrücke **134/C3**
Ludwigstraße **127/E1**
Lueg ins Land **127/F5**
Luise-Kiesselbach-Platz **132/C6**
Luisenstraße **126/A3–133/F2**
Luitpoldbrücke (Prinzregenten-
  brücke) **135/D1**
Luitpoldstraße **126/A3–134/A2**

M
Maderbräustraße **127/E4**
Maffeistraße **127/D3**
Maillingerstraße **133/E1**
Mainzer Straße **130/C3**
Maistraße **133/F4**
Mandlstraße **131/D5**
Mannhardtstraße **127/F5**
Marbachstraße **133/D6**
Margaretenstraße **133/D5**
Maria-Einsiedel-Berg **136/C3**
Maria-Einsiedel-Straße **136/C3**
Mariahilfplatz **134/C4**
Mariannenplatz **134/C2**
Maria-Ward-Straße **128/B4**
Marienplatz **127/D4**
Marienstraße **127/E4**
Marsplatz **129/E6**
Marsstraße **131/E1**
Marstallplatz **127/E3**
Marstallstraße **127/E3**
Martin-Greif-Straße **133/E2**
Martin-Luther-Straße **134/C6**
Maßmannstraße **129/E4**
Mathildenstraße **126/A5–134/A2**
Matthias-Pschorr-Straße **133/E3**
Mauerkircherstraße **131/E6**
Max-Born-Straße **128/C1**
Maxburgstraße **126/B3–134/B2**
Maximiliansbrücke **135/D2**
Maximiliansplatz **126/C2–134/B2**
Maximilianstraße **127/E3**
Max-Joseph-Brücke **131/D6**
Max-Joseph-Platz **127/E3**
Max-Joseph-Straße **126/C2–134/B1**
Max-Planck-Straße **135/D2**
Max-Weber-Platz **135/D2**
Mazaristraße **127/D4**
Meillerweg **135/D3**
Meindlstraße **133/D5**
Melusinenstraße **135/F5**
Menzinger Straße **128/A4**
Metzstraße **135/D3**
Miesingstraße **136/C3**
Milchstraße **135/D3**
Möhlstraße **135/D2**
Montgelasstraße **131/E6**
Moosacher Straße **129/E1**
Morassistraße **127/F6**
Mozartstraße **133/F3**
Mühlbaurstraße **135/E2**
Mühldorfstraße **135/E3**
Müllerstraße **126/B6–134/B3**
Münchner Freiheit **130/C4**
Münzstraße **127/E4**
Murnauer Straße **132/C6**

N
Naupliastraße **137/E3**
Nederlinger Platz **128/C4**
Nederlinger Straße **128/B3**
Neherstraße **135/E2**
Netzerstraße **128/B2**
Neufriedenheimer Straße **132/A6**
Neuhauser Straße **126/B3–134/B2**
Neumarkter Straße **135/F3**
Neureutherstraße **130/B5**
Neuturmstraße **127/E4**
Nibelungenstraße **128/B6**
Nieserstraße **127/D5**
Nikolaistraße **130/C5**
Nordendstraße **130/B5**
Nördliche Auffahrtsallee **128/B5**
Nördliches Schloßrondell **128/B5**
Normannenplatz **131/F5**
Notburgastraße **128/B5**
Nußbaumstraße **126/A6–133/F3**
Nymphenburger Straße **128/C5**

O
Oberanger **126/C5–134/B3**
Oberbiberger Straße **137/F4**
Oberföhringer Straße **131/E6**
Oberländerstraße **133/E5**
Odeonsplatz **127/D2**
Oettingenstraße **135/D2**
Ohlmüllerstraße **134/C4**
Ohmstraße **130/C5**
Opitzstraße **131/F4**
Orlandostraße **127/E4**
Orleansplatz **135/E3**
Orleansstraße **135/D4**
Orpheusstraße **129/D3**
Oskar-von-Miller-Ring **127/D2**
Osterwaldstraße **131/D4**
Ottobrunner Straße **135/F6**
Ottostraße **126/B3–134/B2**

P
Pacellistraße **126/C3–134/B2**
Paradiesstraße **131/D6**
Pariser Platz **135/D3**
Pariser Straße **135/D4**
Partnachplatz **132/C5**
Parzivalplatz **130/C3**
Parzivalstraße **130/B3**
Passauerstraße **133/D6**
Paul-Heyse-Straße **133/F3**
Paul-Heyse-Unterführung **133/F2**
Pelkovenstraße **128/B2**
Perlacher Straße **134/C6**
Perusastraße **127/D3**
Pestalozzistraße **134/A4**
Peter-Auzinger-Straße **137/F2**
Petersplatz **127/D4**
Pettenbeckstraße **127/D4**
Pettenkoferstraße **133/F3**
Petuelring **129/F2**
Petueltunnel **130/B2**
Pfarrstraße **134/C2**
Pfeuferstraße **133/D4**
Pfisterstraße **127/E3**
Pflugstraße **127/E5**
Pfrontener Platz **132/B4**
Pienzenauerstraße **131/E6**
Pilgersheimer Straße **134/B6**
Piusplatz **135/F4**
Platz der Freiheit **129/D5**

Platz der Opfer des National-
  sozialismus **126/C2**
Platzl **127/E4**
Plinganserstraße **133/E6**
Poccistraße **133/E4**
Pognerstraße **136/C2**
Possartstraße **135/E2**
Potsdamer Straße **130/C3**
Prälat-Miller-Weg **127/D4**
Prälat-Zistl-Straße **127/D5**
Prannerstraße **126/C3–134/B2**
Preßburger Straße **132/B5**
Preysingplatz **135/D3**
Preysingstraße **135/D3**
Prielmayerstraße **126/A3–133/F2**
Prinz-Ludwig-Straße **126/C1–134/B1**
Prinzregentenbrücke (Luitpol-
  dbrücke) **135/D1**
Prinzregentenplatz **135/E2**
Prinzregentenstraße **134/C1**
Prof.-Huber-Platz **130/C6**
Promenadeplatz **126/C3–134/B2**
Pullacher Platz **136/C2**
Pullacher Platz **136/C2**
Pütrichstraße **135/D3**

Q
Quellenstraße **134/C4**

R
Rablstraße **135/D4**
Radlkoferstraße **133/E4**
Radlsteg **127/E5**
Raintaler Straße **134/C6**
Ratzingerplatz **136/A3**
Ratzingerplatz **136/A3**
Regerstraße **134/C5**
Reichenbachbrücke **134/C4**
Reichenbachplatz **127/D6**
Reisingerstraße **134/A3**
Reitmorstraße **135/D2**
Renatastraße **128/C5**
Residenzstraße **127/E3**
Rheinbergerstraße **127/D1**
Rheinstraße **130/C4**
Richard-Strauss-Straße **135/F2**
Richard-Wagner-Straße **130/A6**
Ridlerstraße **133/D2**
Riedlstraße (1) **131/D6**
Rindermarkt **127/D5**
Ringseisstraße **133/F3**
Robert-Koch-Straße **135/D2**
Rochusberg **126/C3**
Rochusstraße **126/C3–134/B2**
Roecklplatz **134/A5**
Romanplatz **128/B5**
Romanstraße **128/B5**
Rondell Neuwittelsbach **128/C5**
Röntgenstraße **135/E1**
Rosa-Luxemburg-Platz **129/E4**
Rosenbuschstraße **135/D1**
Rosenheimer Platz **135/D3**
Rosenheimer Straße **134/C3**
Rosenstraße **127/D4**
Rosental **127/D4**
Roßmarkt **126/C6–134/B3**
Rothmundstraße (11) **126/A6**
Rotkreuzplatz **129/D6**
Rottmannstraße **129/F6**
Rückertstraße **133/F3**
Ruffinistraße **129/D5**

STREET ATLAS INDEX

Rümannstraße **130/B2**
Rumfordstraße **127/D5**
Rundfunkplatz **133/F1**
Rupert-Mayer-Straße **136/B3**
Ruppertstraße **133/F4**

S
Säbener Straße **137/F3**
Sachsenstraße **134/B5**
Salvatorplatz **127/D2**
Salvatorstraße **127/D3**
Sanatoriumsplatz **137/D4**
Sankt-Anna-Platz **134/C2**
Sankt-Anna-Straße **127/F2**
Sankt-Bonifatius-Straße **134/C5**
Sankt-Ingbert-Straße **135/D5**
Sankt-Jakobs-Platz **126/C5**
Sankt-Magnus-Straße **137/E3**
Sankt-Martins-Platz **134/C5**
Sankt-Martin-Straße **134/C5**
Sankt-Paul-Straße **133/F3**
Sattlerstraße (7) **126/C4**
Schäfflerstraße **127/D3**
Schäftlarnstraße **136/C2**
Scheidplatz **130/B3**
Scheinerstraße **135/E1**
Schellingstraße **129/F5**
Schenkendorfstraße **130/C2**
Schillerstraße **126/A6–133/F3**
Schleibingerstraße **135/D3**
Schleißheimer Straße **129/F6**
Schlierseestraße **135/D5**
Schlosserstraße **126/A4–134/A2**
Schmidstraße **126/C5**
Schmiedberg **136/C3**
Schneckenburgerstraße **135/E2**
Schönfeldstraße **127/E1**
Schönstraße **137/D2**
Schrammerstraße **127/D3**
Schraudolphstraße **130/B6**
Schulstraße **129/D6**
Schützenstraße **126/A3–133/F2**
Schwanseestraße **135/D6**
Schwanthalerstraße **133/E2**
Schweigerstraße **134/C4**
Schwere-Reiter-Straße **129/E5**
Schwester-Eubulina-Platz **135/D4**
Schyrenplatz **134/B4**
Sebastiansplatz **127/D5**
Sedanstraße **135/D3**
Seidlstraße **133/F1**
Seitzstraße **127/F3**
Sendlinger Kirchplatz **133/E5**
Sendlinger Straße **126/C5–134/B3**
Sendlinger-Tor-Platz **126/B5–133/F2**
Senefelderstraße **126/A4–133/F2**
Seybothstraße **137/D4**
Shakespeareplatz **135/E1**
Siebenbrunner Straße **137/D3**
Siegenburger Straße **132/C3**
Siegesstraße **130/C5**
Siegfriedstraße **130/C4**
Siemensallee **136/A4**
Siglstraße **132/B3**
Sigmundstraße **137/F2**
Silberhornstraße **134/C5**
Simeonstraße **129/D5**
Simon-Knoll-Platz **135/D4**
Singlspielerstraße **126/C5–134/B3**
Sommerstraße **134/B5**
Sonnenstraße **126/B4–134/A2**

Sophienstraße **126/A2–134/A2**
Soyerhofstraße **137/F2**
Sparkassenstraße **127/E4**
Spiridon-Louis-Ring **129/E3**
Sporerstraße **127/D4**
Stachus (Karlsplatz) **126/B3–134/A2**
Steinbeisplatz **132/B4**
Steinheilstraße **130/A6**
Steinsdorfstraße **127/F6**
Steinstraße **135/D3**
Stephansplatz **126/B6**
Stephanstraße **126/B6**
Sterneckerstraße **127/E5**
Sternstraße **135/D2**
Sternwartstraße **135/E1**
Steubenplatz **128/C6**
Stiglmaierplatz **129/F6**
Stollbergstraße **127/F4**
Straubinger Straße **132/C2**
Stuntzstraße **135/F1**
Südliche Auffahrtsallee **128/B5**
Südliches Schloßrondell **128/B5**

T
Tal **127/E4**
Tassiloplatz **135/D4**
Tattenbachstraße **135/D2**
Tegelbergstraße **137/E3**
Tegernseer Landstraße **134/C6**
Tegernseer Platz **134/C5**
Tengstraße **130/B5**
Thalkirchner Brücke **136/C2**
Thalkirchner Platz **136/C2**
Thalkirchner Straße **133/E6**
Theatinerstraße **127/D3**
Theklastraße **127/D6**
Theodolindenstraße **137/D4**
Theodorparkstraße **131/D6**
Therese-Studer-Straße **130/A4**
Theresienhöhe **133/E4**
Theresienstraße **130/A6**
Thiereckstraße **127/D4**
Thierschstraße **127/F5**
Thomasiusplatz **135/E5**
Thomas-Wimmer-Ring **127/F5**
Tierparkstraße **137/D2**
Tiroler Platz **137/E3**
Tivolistraße **131/D6**
Tizianplatz **128/B5**
Tizianstraße **128/C4**
Trappentreustraße **133/D2**
Trappentreutunnel **133/D2**
Treffauerstraße **132/C5**
Triebstraße **128/C1**
Triftstraße **135/D2**
Tübinger Straße **132/C3**
Tulbeckstraße **133/D2**
Tumblingerstraße **133/F4**
Türkenstraße **126/C2–134/B1**

U
Uhlandstraße **133/F3**
Ungererstraße **130/C4**
Unsöldstraße **127/F2**
Unterer Anger **126/C6–134/B3**
Untermenzinger Straße **128/A2**
Utzschneiderstraße **127/D5**

V
Valleystraße **133/E5**
Veterinärstraße **130/C6**

Viktoriaplatz **130/C4**
Viktoriastraße **130/C4**
Viktualienmarkt **127/D5**
Virchowstraße **130/C3**
Viscardigasse (Drückeberger-Gassl) **127/D3**
Vogelweideplatz **135/F2**
Volkartstraße **129/D5**
Volpinistraße **128/B4**
Von-der-Tann-Straße **127/E1**

W
Wackersberger Straße **133/E5**
Wagmüllerstraße **134/C1**
Waisenhausstraße **129/D4**
Waldfriedhofstraße **132/A6**
Wallstraße **126/B5**
Waltherstraße **133/F3**
Wartburgplatz **130/C2**
Washingtonstraße **128/C6**
Wedekindplatz **131/D4**
Weinstraße **127/D4**
Weißenburger Platz **135/D3**
Weißenburger Straße **135/D3**
Weißenfelderplatz **132/B3**
Welfenstraße **134/C4**
Werdenfelsstraße **132/B5**
Werinherstraße **134/C5**
Werneckstraße **131/D5**
Westendstraße **132/B4**
Westenriederstraße **127/E5**
Westermühlstraße **134/B3**
Wettersteinplatz **134/B6**
Widenmayerstraße **135/D2**
Wiener Platz **135/D3**
Wilhelm-Hale-Straße **128/C6**
Wilhelmstraße **130/C5**
Willi-Gebhardt-Ufer **129/E3**
Wilramstraße **135/E5**
Winckelstraße **134/A3**
Windenmacherstraße **127/D3**
Winthirplatz **128/C6**
Wintrichring **128/B4**
Winzererstraße **129/F5**
Wittelsbacherbrücke **134/B4**
Wittelsbacherplatz **127/D2**
Wittelsbacherstraße **134/A5**
Wolfratshauser Straße **136/A6**
Wörthstraße **135/D3**
Wotanstraße **128/A6**
Wredestraße **133/E1**
Wurzerstraße **127/F3**

Z
Zamboninistraße **128/B5**
Zaubzerstraße **135/E2**
Zellstraße **135/D3**
Zenettistraße **133/F4**
Zentnerstraße **130/A5**
Zentralländstraße **136/C4**
Zeppelinstraße **134/C4**
Zieblandstraße **130/A5**
Ziemssenstraße **126/A5–134/A3**
Zillertalstraße **132/C5**
Zschokkestraße **132/B3**
Zuccalistraße **128/A6**
Zugspitzstraße **134/C5**
Zumpestraße **135/E2**
Zweibrückenstraße **127/F5**
Zweigstraße **126/A4–134/A2**
Zwingerstraße (14) **127/E5**

KEY TO STREET ATLAS

Motorway with number
Autobahn mit Nummer
Autoroute avec numéro

Motorway junction number
Nummer der Autobahnanschlussstelle
Numéro d'echangeur d'autoroute

Expressway/ Federal road
Schnellstraße/ Bundesstraße
Route express/ Route nationale

Main through road
Durchgangsstraße
Grande route

Other roads/ Footpath
Übrige Straßen/ Weg
Autres routes/ Sentier

Roads under construction/ projected
Straßen in Bau/ Planung
Routes en construction/ en projet

Pedestrian zone/ One-way street
Fußgängerzone/ Einbahnstraße
Zone piétonnière/ Rue à sens unique

Town and communal boundary
Stadt- und Gemeindegrenze
Limite de ville et commune

Environmental zone
Umweltzone
Zone environnement

Railway with station
Eisenbahn mit Bahnhof
Voie ferrée avec gare

Freight and industrial railway
Güter- und Industriebahn
Voie ferrée de marchandise et industrielle

Rapid transit train with number and station
S-Bahn mit Nummer und Station
Train en trafic suburbain avec numéro et gare

Underground/ Light Rail
U-Bahn/ Stadtbahn
Métro/ Métro Léger

Bus/ Tramway with terminus
Bus/ Straßenbahn mit Endhaltestelle
Autobus/ Tramway avec terminus

Car park/ Parking house/ Under-
ground car park
Parkplatz/ Parkhaus/ Tiefgarage
Parking/ Garage/ Parking souterrain

Park+Ride/ Parking control system
Park+Ride/ Parkleitsystem
Park+Ride/ Système de signalisation

Walking tours
Stadtspaziergänge
Promenades en ville

Indoor swimming pool
Hallenbad
Piscine couverte

Church
Kirche
Église

Hospital
Krankenhaus
Hôpital

Camping site/ Youth hostel
Campingplatz/ Jugendherberge
Camping/ Auberge de jeunesse

Post office
Post
Bureau de poste

Forester's lodge
Försterei
Maison forestière

Isolated trees
Einzelne Bäume
Arbres isolés

Inn/ Excursion-Inn
Wirtshaus/ Ausflugslokal
Auberge/ Café-Restaurant

Transmitting station/ Lighthouse
Sendeanlage/ Leuchtturm
Station d'émission/ Phare

Monument/ Tower
Denkmal/ Turm
Monument/ Tour

Windmill/ Windpower
Windmühle/ Windrad
Moulin à vent/ Éolienne

Tourist information center
Tourist-Information
Syndicat d'initiative

Consulate/ Embassy
Konsulat/ Botschaft
Consulat/ Ambassade

Forest/ Park, Cemetery
Wald/ Park, Friedhof
Forêt/ Parc, Cimetière

Vineyard
Weinberg
Vignoble

Heath/ Marsh, Swamp
Heide/ Moor, Sumpf
Lande/ Marais, Marécage

MARCO POLO Highlights

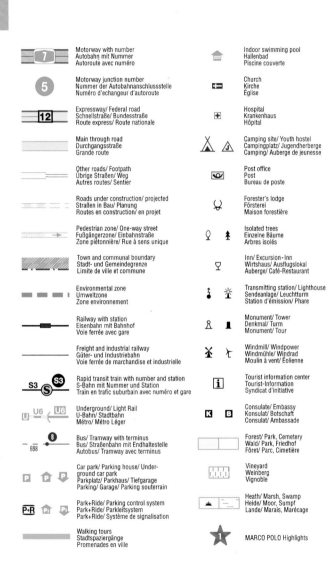

INDEX

This index lists all sights and destinations, plus the names of important people, streets, places and key words featured in this guide. Numbers in **bold** indicate a main entry; numbers in *italics* refer to illustrations.

Allianz Arena 6, *7*, *18*, 20, **56**
Alte Pinakothek **43**, 49, 105
Alter Peter, see: Peterskirche
Altes Rathaus (Old Town Hall) 28, 102
Amalienburg 55
Amalienstraße 74
Antikensammlung 46, 105
Architekturgalerie München 107
Asamkirche **29**
Asampassage 74
Au **50**
Auer Dult 4, 110
Augustinerkeller 18, **62**
Badenburg 55
Bamberger Haus 47
Bavaria 7, **56**
Bavaria-Filmgelände 8, **57**
Bayerische Rückversicherung 106
Bayerisches Nationalmuseum **39**, 105
Beer **21**, 61, 115
Beer gardens 18, **61**
Bernheimer Palais 33
BMW-Hochhaus 57, 105
BMW-Welt/BMW-Museum **57**, 105
Botanischer Garten (Botanical Garden) 53
Brunnenhof 26
Bürgersaalkirche 29
Chinesischer Turm (Chinese Tower) 7, 25, 45, 62, 106
Cuvilliés Theater **91**
Dachau (Concentration Camp) **58**
Deutsches Museum 8, 50, **51**, 57, 107, 108, 115
Deutsches Theater 91
Dreifaltigkeitskirche 30
Eisbach 17, 20, 23, 45
Englischer Garten (English Garden) 4, 6, 9, *12*, 20, 25, 39, **44**, 62, 100, 105, 106, 115
FC Bayern München 20, 34, 52, 56, 112
Feldherrnhalle (Field Marshals' Hall) 31
Filmmuseum 111
Fischbrunnen 34, 107
Flaucher 9, **58**
Floßlände Thalkirchen 20, **58**
Flugwerft Schleißheim 57
Football arena (TSV 1860/ Grünwalder Straße) 17
Frauenkirche (Cathedral Church of Our Lady) 28, **31**, 38, 103
Fünf Höfe 8, 24, 72, 73, **79**
Gärtnerplatz 7, 12, 50, **52**
Gärtnerplatz district 74
Gasteig 5, 51, **52**, 89
Giesing 17
Glockenbach district 25, **50**, 83, 88
Glockenspiel 24
Glyptothek 9, **46**, 105

Haidhausen **50**, 74, 83
Haus der Kunst **39**, 105
Heiliggeistkirche 32
Herkulessaal **88**
Herz-Jesu-Kirche 53
Hofbräuhaus 14, 28, **70**, 103, 148
Hofbräukeller 62
Hofgarten (Court Garden) 5, 6, 24, 25, **40**, 65
Hohenzollernstraße 74
Hypo-Hochhaus 106
Isar (river) 9, 13, **20**, *26*, 50, 51, 100, 107
Isartor (Isar Gate) 41, 104, 115
Isartorplatz 41
Jagd und Fischereimuseum (Hunting and Fishing Museum) 102
Japanisches Teehaus 4, **45**
Jüdisches Museum **33**
Karlsplatz, see: Stachus
Karlstor 33
Kaufingerstraße 24, 28, 72, 102
Kinderreich ('Kids' Kingdom', Deutsches Museum) 107, **108**
Kinder und Jugendmuseum 108
Kleinhesseloher See (pond) 44, **45**, 63
Königlicher Hirschgarten 62
Königsplatz **46**, 105
Kunstareal 104
Künstlerhaus 33
KZ-Gedenkstätte Dachau, see: Dachau
Lake Starnberg, see: Starnberger See
Lehel 39
Lenbachbrunnen 33
Lenbachhaus **46**, 105
Lenbachplatz **33**, 65
Leopoldstraße **46**, 74
Löwenbräukeller 62
Ludwigskirche 47
Ludwigstraße **47**, 50
Luitpoldpark **47**
Mae West sculpture 106
Magdalenenklause 55
Marienplatz 9, 11, 12, 21, 24, 26, 28, **34**, 36, 72, 73, 102, 107, 148
Mariensäule 34, 102, 107
Marstallmuseum 55
Maximilianeum 34, **58**, 115
Maximilianshöfe 66, **79**
Maximiliansplatz **85**
Maximilianstraße 26, **34**, *35*, 72, 74, 77
Maxvorstadt 12, 25, **42**, 83
Michaelskirche 35
Monopteros *12*, 25, **45**
Muffatwerk 90
Müllersches Volksbad 9, 50, **52**
Müllerstraße 74
Münchner Freiheit 47, **48**
Münchner Kammerspiele 35

Münchner Kindl 21
Münchner Lustspielhaus 87
Münchner Marionettentheater 107
Münchner Stadtmuseum 8, **35**, 104
Museum Brandhorst 25, 42, **48**, *102*, 105
Museum Mensch und Natur 53
Museumsviertel (museum complex) 25
Nationaltheater (Opera House) 34, 36, *82*, 88
Neue Pinakothek *48*, **49**, 105
Neues Rathaus (New Town Hall) 11, 24, 26, 34, **36**, 102, 104
Neuhausen **52**
Neuhauser Straße 28, 33, 34, 72
Nymphenburg 52
Nymphenburg Palace, see: Schloss Nymphenburg
Nymphenburg Park 27, *124*
Odeonsplatz 25, 26, 31, 73
Oktoberfest 7, 12, 21, **22**, 23, 56, 92, 110, 111, 112, 113, 148
Old Town 12, **27**
Olympia Alm 4, **59**
Olympiaberg 4, 15, **59**
Olympiagelände (Olympic Site) 6, 26, 47, 56, **58**, 78, 105, 111
Olympiaturm 58
Olympic Park 4, 6, **58**, 111
Olympic Stadium 7, 15, **58**, 105
Opera House, see: Nationaltheater
Ost-West-Friedenskirche 59
Pagodenburg 55
Pasinger Fabrik 89
Peterskirche (St Peter's Church/Old Peter) 12, 24, **37**, 104, 107
Pinakothek der Moderne 25, 42, **49**, 105
Pini Haus 33
Porzellanmuseum 55
Prinzregentenstraße 39
Prinzregententheater 88
Rathausturm 21, 102
Residenz 25, 26, **37**, 88
Residenztheater **91**
Rindermarkt 104
Rockmuseum 58
Schauburg 108
Schauspielhaus 91
Schellingstraße 74
Schlachthof Wirtshaus & Bühne 87
Schlosskanal 52, **55**
Schloss Nymphenburg 38, 52, **54**, 55, 115
Schwabing 12, **42**, 74, 83, 88
Sea Life **109**, 117
Seehaus 45, **63**
Sendlinger Straße 74
Siegestor 47
Sonnenstraße 14, 16, 25, 82, **86**
Spielzeugmuseum (Toy Museum) **29**, 102

Staatliches Museum Ägyptischer Kunst 42, **49**, 105
Staatstheater am Gärtnerplatz 52
Stachus 28, **33**, 72, 73, 82
St Anna im Lehel 41
Starnberg 17
Starnberger See 17
Südfriedhof 52
Tal 74
Thalkirchen 56
Theatinerkirche 24, 27, **38**, 47

Theatinerstraße 24, 28, 72, 73
Theatron 26, 59
Theresienwiese 7, 12, 14, **56**, 110, 111
Tierpark Hellabrunn (zoo) 56, **109**, 110
Tollwood Festival 14, 57, 111
TSV 1860 München 20, 34, 56
Türkenstraße 25, 74
University 50
Valentin-Karlstadt-Musäum **42**, 104

Viktualienmarkt 11, 24, 26, 28, **79**, 104, 107, 115
Volkssternwarte (Observatory) 109
Volkstheater 91
Waldwirtschaft 63
Wappenhaus 52, 53
Westend 12, 74, 83
Westpark 6, **78**
Wiesn, see: Oktoberfest
Zeiss Planetarium 51

WRITE TO US

e-mail: info@marcopologuides.co.uk

Did you have a great holiday?
Is there something on your mind?
Whatever it is, let us know!
Whether you want to praise, alert us to errors or give us a personal tip – MARCO POLO would be pleased to hear from you.
We do everything we can to provide the very latest information for your trip.

Nevertheless, despite all of our authors' thorough research, errors can creep in. MARCO POLO does not accept any liability for this. Please contact us by e-mail or post.

MARCO POLO Travel Publishing Ltd
Pinewood, Chineham Business Park
Crockford Lane, Chineham
Basingstoke, Hampshire RG24 8AL
United Kingdom

PICTURE CREDITS
Cover photograph: Theatiner Church, Café Tambosi, Odeonsplatz (Look: Zegers)
Charlie: Benjamin Röder, 2010 (17 bottom); W. Dieterich (14/15, 62, 112 top); DuMont Bildarchiv: Kluyver (9, 79); Grillionaire GmbH: Stefan Bogner (16 centre); Huber: Kolley (36), Radelt (front flap right), Römmelt (55), Schmid (2 bottom, 12/13, 18/19, 21, 37, 47, 60/61, 69, 70, 90); Laif: Haenel (25, 50), Huber (6), Kerber (84, 106), Madej (8), Riehle (107); Laif/GAFF: Adenis (31); Laif/hemis.fr: Mailsant (94); Look: age fotostock (10/11, 145), Greune (53), TerraVista (59, 110/111), Wothe (44/45), Zegers (1top); mauritius images: Imagebroker.net (4), Kolley (24 top), Protzel (24 bottom, 68 right), Siepmann (42), Widmann (48/49); mauritius images/imagebroker: Obermeier (111), Siepmann (110); Benjamin Antony Monn (16 bottom); Niederlassung: Alexander Schwarz (16 top); D. Simon (3 top, 72/73, 108); T. Stankiewicz (front flap left, 2 top, 2 centre top, 2 centre bottom, 3 centre bottom, 4, 5, 7, 22, 26/27, 32, 35, 38, 41, 56, 57, 65, 66, 67, 68 left, 74, 81, 92/93, 97, 98, 101, 102/103, 104, 112 bottom, 113, 120/121); P. Stengelin (86/87); SUP-Academy: Stephan Gölnitz (17 top); vario images: imagebroker (3 centre, 76, 82/83, 89, 109)

1st Edition 2013
Worldwide Distribution: Marco Polo Travel Publishing Ltd, Pinewood, Chineham Business Park, Crockford Lane, Chineham, Basingstoke, Hampshire RG24 8AL, United Kingdom. Email: sales@marcopolouk.com
© MAIRDUMONT GmbH & Co. KG, Ostfildern
Chief editors: Michaela Lienemann (concept, managing editor), Marion Zorn (concept, text editor)
Author: Karl Forster; co-author: Amadeus Danesitz, Dr. Astrid Dobmeier, Alex Wulkow; editor: Ulrike Frühwald
Programme supervision: Ann-Katrin Kutzner, Nikolai Michaelis, Silwen Randebrock
Picture editors: Gabriele Forst, Barbara Schmid
What's hot: wunder media, Munich
Cartography street atlas & pull-out map: © MAIRDUMONT, Ostfildern
Design: milchhof: atelier, Berlin; Front cover, page 1, pull-out map cover: factor product munich
Translated from German by Christopher Wynne; editor of the English edition: Christopher Wynne
Prepress: M. Feuerstein, Wigel
Phrase book in cooperation with Ernst Klett Sprachen GmbH, Stuttgart, Editorial by Pons Wörterbücher

DOS & DON'TS ☝

How to spare yourself trials and tribulations

DON'T DRIVE AROUND MUNICH

Even if you've driven around Naples or Paris, leave your car in the hotel carpark or on the edge of town (but take your luggage with you). Driving in Munich – especially in the rush hour – is like a fight to the death. Plus the fact that there are hardly enough parking spaces for local residents, so that you're forced to park illegally. Unfortunately, most people seem to think that the law of the road means charging around and ignoring everyone else. At traffic lights, you start moving off as soon as it turns orange and, conversely, you don't stop at orange but put your foot on the accelerator instead. Courtesy and consideration slow down the flow of the traffic – or so a few black sheep seem to think – and they're the ones who try to dictate what happens on the roads. Illegal parking will cost you at least 15 euros; if you're obstructing something, your car will be towed away – and that will set you back at least 150 euros, plus a taxi fare.

DON'T ARGUE WITH THE POLICE

Munich's 'boys in green' have the reputation of being easy-going and even turn a blind eye occasionally. If you find the right tone of voice, you'll probably find they're very fair. If you carry on insisting that, under no circumstances whatsoever, could the traffic light have been red, then you'll most likely lose your driving licence before you've even finished your long-winded explanation.

DON'T SPEAK IN DIALECT

Don't try to learn Bavarian. It sounds terrible and the locals won't think it's funny either. When non-Bavarians say pfiadi – which means 'good-bye' – it always sound wrong, as do other attempts at pronouncing regional words. Just stick to standard German if you can. Everything else is simply awful.

DON'T CRITICISE MUNICH

Don't tell the locals how much more beautiful, more elegant or how much more fun it is in Hamburg, Berlin, Paris, New York or anywhere else for that matter. Just remember: the people of Munich are entitled to run their own city down as much as they like, but tourists are expected to marvel at everything.

DON'T LOOK FOR TOO MUCH 'GENUINE' FOLKSINESS

It's best to avoid such traditional tourist honeypots such as the Hofbräuhaus or Marienplatz at noon – unless you like being with crowds of fellow tourists goggling at the glockenspiel. Come back again in the evening at 5pm when there are more locals around.

DON'T GO TO THE OKTOBERFEST ON A SATURDAY

At weekends, the place is inundated with people. It's virtually impossible to get into one of the tents even in the afternoon as they usually close their doors early to avoid overcrowding. It's much better to plan your visit for during the week.